THERE IS NO
ZOO IN
ZOOLOGY

THERE IS NO
ZOO IN
ZOOLOGY

AND OTHER BEASTLY
MISPRONUNCIATIONS

*An Opinionated Guide for
the Well-Spoken*

Charles Harrington Elster

COLLIER BOOKS
MACMILLAN PUBLISHING COMPANY
New York
COLLIER MACMILLAN PUBLISHERS
London

Collier Books
Macmillan Publishing Company
866 Third Avenue, New York, NY 10022
Collier Macmillan Canada, Inc.

Library of Congress Cataloging-in-Publication Data

Elster, Charles Harrington.
    There is no zoo in zoology, and other beastly mispronunciations.

    1. English language—United States—Pronunciation.
I. Title.
PE2815.E55   1988   428.1   88-12949
ISBN 0-02-031830-8

The author gratefully acknowledges the following publishers for permission to excerpt from their copyrighted works:

   Charles Scribner's Sons, Publishers, an imprint of Macmillan Publishing Company: Sidney I. Landau, excerpted from *Dictionaries: The Art and Craft of Lexicography*. Copyright © 1984 Sidney I. Landau.
   Harper & Row, Publishers, Inc.: Excerpts from Edwin Newman's introduction to the *NBC Handbook of Pronunciation*, 4th ed., by Eugene Ehrlich and Raymond Hand, Jr. Copyright © 1984 by Harper & Row, Publishers, Inc. Introduction copyright © 1984 by Harper & Row, Publishers, Inc.
   Merriam-Webster Inc.: Excerpts from *Webster's New International Dictionary*, 2d ed., copyright © 1941 by Merriam-Webster Inc. Excerpts from *Webster's Ninth New Collegiate Dictionary*, copyright © 1988 by Merriam-Webster Inc. Excerpts from *A Pronouncing Dictionary of American English* by John Samuel Kenyon and Thomas Albert Knott, copyright © 1953 by Merriam-Webster Inc. By permission of Merriam-Webster Inc., publishers of the Merriam-Webster® dictionaries.
   Oxford University Press: Excerpts from *The Oxford English Dictionary*, copyright © 1971 by Oxford University Press. Excerpts from *A Dictionary of Modern English Usage* by H. W. Fowler, copyright © 1961 by Oxford University Press.
   Random House, Inc.: Excerpts from *The Random House Dictionary of the English Language*, 2d ed.—unabridged. Copyright © 1987 by Random House, Inc.
   Simon & Schuster, Inc.: Excerpts from *Webster's New World Guide to Pronunciation* by William S. Chisholm, Jr. Copyright © 1984 by Simon & Schuster, Inc.

Designed by Nancy Sugihara

Printed in the United States of America

There Is No Zoo in Zoology is also available in a hardcover edition from Macmillan Publishing Company

---

Acknowledgments

It is rare that one writes a book without the aid and encouragement of others. I wish to thank Dr. Pat Launer of San Diego State University for her very clever suggestions; my editor, Philip Turner, for his enthusiasm and clearheaded advice; my agent, Bill Gladstone of Waterside Productions, for his confidence and persistence; Dr. Merrilee Antrim of San Diego Mesa College; the Writers' Bookstore and Haven of San Diego; and my wife, Myrna Zambrano, for believing in me.

To my parents,
Nancy and Reinhardt Elster,
with gratitude and love.

Contents

Preface

From an early age, my omnierudite mother impressed upon me the importance of pronunciation. She taught me that the well-spoken person, whatever his opinions, will be well-received, while the poor speaker will be scorned like a dinner guest who mishandles his silverware and wipes his mouth on his sleeve.

My mother was always right about pronunciation, and if anyone in the family mispronounced a word, she would not fail to point it out—during dinner, during an argument, even while we were on the phone. On a table in the living room lay the family dictionary—*Webster's New International*, 2d ed. —to which she would send us for confirmation if we tried to put up a fight. This tome was the ultimate authority in our disputes, which of course she always won. Though we never saw her studying it, we figured she had that great book memorized.

As I got older it became harder and harder to accept her admonishment. Once, when I was home from college on vacation, I used the word "flaccid," pronouncing it FLAS-id. She stopped me right away.

"That's FLAK-sid, dear," she called from the kitchen.

"Oh, come on, Mom, you're kidding. Nobody says it that way."

"Well, *I* say it that way, and that's the proper way to pronounce it."

"But my English professor doesn't pronounce it that way."

"Then your English professor is wrong."

My professor, wrong? Such hubris must be punished, I thought. I marched off to the dictionary, fully expecting to return triumphant and rub her nose in the page. Instead I found that my professor and I and scores of other smart folks I knew were indeed wrong. The pronunciation FLAK-sid stared limply back at me; FLAS-id was nowhere to be found. I was mortified, and from that day I vowed I would out-mother my mother if it took a lifetime.

Several years ago, while working as an editor of educational software, I was fortunate to be able to spend many, many hours poring over numerous dictionaries, studying the definitions, derivations, and pronunciations of thousands of English words. As I went along I came across dozens for which my sources preferred a pronunciation different from the one I used or was accustomed to hearing. It was then that I began to collect the entries that appear in this book.

Here you will find about four hundred mostly common words that are frequently and flagrantly mispronounced—not only by John Doe but by a great number of well-educated, well-read, professional, and prominent people as well. Many are words I once habitually mispronounced (now I know better), and all are words I have heard mispronounced by otherwise careful speakers from every part of the country.

Like usage, pronunciation has and will continue to change, but the change is not always the result of normal evolution. Often it is ill-considered, illogical, and unnecessary. In some cases, new pronunciations are the whimsical product of a pseudo-sophisticated few, who foist them on a public hungry for a way to sound more cultivated; in others, educated people with a command of a large vocabulary simply do not bother to check the pronunciation of a word they hear or read or look up in a dictionary. We tend to invent our own pronunciations for words encountered in reading, and model our speech after those "whose abilities and character entitle [their] opinions to respect," as Noah Webster wrote, "but whose pronunciation may be altogether accidental or capricious."

We all learn our pronunciation from those around us: parents, relatives, teachers, friends, and broadcasters. These are not always the most reliable sources (not everyone can have my mother). This book offers you an opportunity to relearn your pronunciation from those who know the subject best: the makers of dictionaries and pronunciation guides.

In these pages you will not discover how most Americans pronounce a word, or how a certain privileged class of Americans pronounces a word. You will discover which pronunciations are preferred by most authorities, and which have the longest or strongest tradition in the dictionaries. (Of course, in the process you will also get a healthy dose of my opinions.)

This means that in certain cases this book endorses a pronunciation that is no longer widespread, or one that may not be preferred by your particular dictionary, or one that is not used by the people of your locality. However, bear in mind that it is one that is generally accepted and has been heard in American English over the last hundred years. In other words, no one can legitimately find fault with you for using the pronunciations recommended here.

In selecting the entries for this book, I have been guided by the assumption that a concise collection of everyday words frequently mispronounced would be the most useful resource for the general reader. Therefore, place names are excluded, for advice on them can be found in other, more specific sources. I have also omitted foreign words or expressions, except for those few that dictionaries agree have been absorbed into English and that I have judged to be commonly mispronounced. There are a handful of names of persons, which I have selected as being particularly prone to mispronunciation.

Finally, I have tried to avoid any preference for a particular regional form of speech. No matter how many books of this kind are published, a speaker from Alabama, a speaker from Massachusetts, and a speaker from California will never quite sound the same—and there is no reason why they should. But there is also no reason why they should share the same mispronunciations. That is why I have tried to determine where my sources concur on what might be called a standard, or general, American pronunciation.

A word of caution on improving your speech: If you are the sort of person who believes that good pronunciation will make you seem more intelligent or witty or sophisticated, this book is not for you. Good pronunciation is not something you put on for an occasion like a mask or a suit of fancy clothes, for you can be sure others will see you through your disguise for what you are.

Good pronunciation is cultivated; that is, refined by study and training. It is the hallmark of the person who seeks knowledge for self-improvement, and uses it conscientiously—not to imitate, impress, or intimidate others. Finally, good pronunciation, though in theory a collective concept, is, in essence, an individual matter. It is what seems most natural, as well as proper, to *you*.

That is why I have written this book: to instruct and delight you, whoever you are and whatever you do. Actors, broadcasters, public speakers, and other professionals whose work places particular emphasis on clear and precise communication can benefit from the advice given here. Lovers and watchdogs of the language should also find much of interest in these pages, perhaps even some good grist for their mills. But mainly this book is for any well-read and well-spoken person who thinks and cares about how words are used and pronounced.

I did not write it to change you or the language, or to establish an arbitrary standard to which all must conform. Pronunciation, like politics, is a passionate subject, forever open to interpretation. This book is one man's informed opinion, based on a variety of reliable sources, about a number of controversial words. I present it to you in the hope that it will assist, amuse, enlighten, and inflame you, and give you as much joy and distress in the reading as it did me in the making.

> In words, as fashions, the same rule will hold,
> Alike fantastic, if too new or old;
> Be not the first by whom the new are tried,
> Nor yet the last to lay the old aside.
>
> —ALEXANDER POPE

CHARLES HARRINGTON ELSTER
San Diego, California
April 1988

The Key to Pronunciation

The following key was designed to indicate the majority of English speech sounds in a simple, general, and comprehensible manner. I created it on the assumption that most readers do not enjoy trying to discern and decipher minute, arcane subscript and superscript, and resent having to refer to the key for every word. Therefore, this key employs no signs, symbols, accent marks, or inverted letters; it is not phonetic or diacritical. It is what I call a *literal* key—it relies only upon small and capital letters, combinations of letters, and underscored and boldfaced letters to indicate sound and stress.

No key is perfect, or even comprehensive. All must approximate in some fashion, and this one is no exception. In constructing it I have borrowed from various sources, but the key as a whole is my own, as is the responsibility for any weaknesses it may have.

Vowel Sounds

A

A, a—as in: FLAT, EXACT, PASS, BACK
AH, ah—as in: SPA, FATHER, ODD, NOT
AHR, ahr—as in: CAR, JAR, ALARM
AIR, air—as in: HAIR, STARE, BEAR

AY, ay—as in: HAY, WAIT, CAME, STATE, WHEY

AW, aw—as in: RAW, ALL, WALK

E

E, e—as in: YES, LET, STEP

EE, ee—as in: SEE, BEAT, KEY

EER, eer—as in: PIER, BEER, FEAR

I

I, i—as in: IN, HIT, SIP

Y, y and EYE, eye—as in: BY, NICE, PIE, RIGHT, AISLE
(NOTE: Y is used in combination with other letters to form a syllable: SLYT-lee [slightly]; EYE is used when this sound by itself forms a syllable: EYE-land [island].)

O

OH, oh—as in: GO, SEW, COAT

OO, oo—as in: DO, OOZE, RULE, SOUP

OR, or—as in: FOR, DOOR, BORN, WAR

OOR, oor—as in: POOR, TOUR, LURE

OW, ow—as in: COW, TOWER, OUT, DOUBT

OY, oy—as in: OIL, LOIN, BOY, AHOY

U

UH, uh—as in: UPPER, DULL, SOME, COLOR; also: AGO, ALLOW

UR, ur—as in: TURN, STIR, WERE, LEARN

UU, uu—as in: PULL, FULL, or GOOD, TOOK, WOULD

Obscure, Unstressed, Lightened, or Variable Vowel Sounds

A, a—as in: AGO, FINAL, WOMAN, REPUBLICAN

E, e—as in: ITEM, TAKEN, SHIPMENT, DIFFERENCE

I, i—as in: DIRECT, APRIL, EDIBLE, POLICY, CHARITY

O, o—as in: CONNECT, POLITE, GALLOP, CARROT

U, u—as in: FOCUS, CIRCUS, SINGULAR, LETTUCE

Consonant Sounds

B, b—as in: BOY, CAB, TROUBLE

CH, ch—as in: CHIP, CATCHER, PEACH

D, d—as in: DOG, ADD, SUDDEN

F, f—as in: FAT, EFFORT, STAFF

G, g—as in: GET, BIGGER, BOGUS, TAG

H, h—as in: HIT, HOPE, AHOY, BEHIND

HW, hw—as in: WHEAT, WHALE, WHET

J, j—as in: JUG, JUICE, TRAGIC, AGE

K, k—as in: CUP, KING, TAKE, ACTOR, PACK

L, l—as in: LEG, ALSO, BELL

M, m—as in: MY, HUMBLE, EMBLEM

N, n—as in: NO, KNEE, END, WINNER

NG, ng—as in: SING, ANGER, TANK

P, p—as in: PEN, PEPPER, POP

R, r—as in: RED, ARRIVE, CAR

S, s—as in: SIT, ASK, PASS

SH, sh—as in: SHE, NATION, RUSH

T, t—as in: TOP, BITTER, LIST

TH, th—as in: THIN, NOTHING, BATH

TH, th—as in: THERE, BROTHER, BATHE

V, v—as in: VERY, EVEN, LIVE

W, w—as in: WILL, WAIT, QUIET

Y, y—as in: YES, YOU, UNION

Z, z—as in: ZOO, DAZE, PLEASE

ZH, zh—as in: VISION, MEASURE, AZURE

Stress/Accent

- Syllables are separated by a hyphen [-]. (In this book, words are divided into syllables to approximate the way they are pronounced, not in accordance with standard word division.)
- Syllables printed in CAPITAL letters are accented.
- Syllables printed in small letters are not accented.
- Words of one syllable are printed in CAPITALS.
- Words of two or more syllables, where each syllable receives an equal stress, are printed entirely in CAPITALS: SHORT-LYVD; LAWNG-DRAWN-OUT.
- Words of more than two syllables that have a primary and secondary stress are printed in the following manner: The syllable receiving the secondary stress is printed in CAPITALS, and the syllable receiving the primary stress is printed in **BOLDFACED CAPITALS**: SPAHN-ta-**NEE**-i-tee.

Authorities Consulted

The pronunciations recommended in this book are based upon the opinions of the following authorities (some of which are preceded by the abbreviations used in the text to refer to them):

Worcester

Worcester, Joseph. *A Dictionary of the English Language*. Philadelphia: J. B. Lippincott & Company, 1884. (A revised edition of Worcester's dictionary of 1860.)

Baker, Josephine Turck. *Ten Thousand Words: How to Pronounce Them*. Evanston–Chicago: The Correct English Publishing Company, 1905.

Century

Whitney, William Dwight, and Benjamin E. Smith, eds. *The Century Dictionary*, revised & enlarged edition, 10 vols. New York: The Century Company, 1914. (Compiled from 1889–1914.)

Webster's Collegiate Dictionary. Springfield: G. & C. Merriam Company, 1917.

W. H. P. Phyfe or Phyfe.

Phyfe, W. H. P. *18,000 Words Often Mispronounced*. New York & Chicago: A. L. Burt Company, 1926.

H. W. Fowler or Fowler

Fowler, H. W. *A Dictionary of Modern English Usage*. Oxford: Clarendon Press, 1961. (Originally published in 1926.)

New Century

Emery, H. G., and K. G. Brewster, eds. *The New Century Dictionary*. New York: D. Appleton–Century Company, 1942. (Originally published in 1927.)

OED

Murray, Sir Augustus Henry, et al., eds. *The Oxford English Dictionary*, compact edition, 2 vols. Oxford: Oxford University Press, 1971. (Compiled from 1891 to 1928, with supplement published in 1933.)

Vizetelly, Frank H. *Desk-Book of Twenty-five Thousand Words Frequently Mispronounced,* fourth edition. New York: Grosset & Dunlap, 1929.

Webster 2

Webster's New International Dictionary, second edition. Springfield: G. & C. Merriam Company, 1941. (Originally published in 1934.)

Gilmartin, John G. *Everyday Errors in Pronunciation.* New York: Walter J. Black, Inc., 1936.

Witherspoon, Alexander M. *Common Errors in English and How to Avoid Them.* New Jersey: Littlefield, Adams & Co., 1983. (Originally published by Copeland & Lamm, Inc., New York., 1943.)

American College

The American College Encyclopedic Dictionary. Chicago: Spencer Press, Inc., 1953. (First published in 1947.)

Kenyon and Knott

Kenyon, John Samuel, and Thomas Albert Knott. *A Pronouncing Dictionary of American English.* Springfield: G. & C. Merriam Company, 1949. (First published in 1944.)

The Winston Dictionary, advanced edition. Philadelphia: The John C. Winston Company, 1951.

Webster 3

Webster's Third New International Dictionary. Springfield: G. & C. Merriam Company, 1961.

Funk & Wagnalls New Practical Standard Dictionary. New York: Funk & Wagnalls Company, 1962.

American Heritage, New College

The American Heritage Dictionary, new college edition. Boston: Houghton Mifflin Company, 1982. (Originally published in 1969.)

The New Merriam-Webster Pocket Dictionary. Springfield: G. & C. Merriam Company, 1971.

Scribner–Bantam

The Scribner–Bantam English Dictionary. New York: Bantam Books, 1979.

Funk & Wagnalls Standard

Funk & Wagnalls Standard Dictionary. New York: Lippincott & Crowell, 1980.

Oxford American

The Oxford American Dictionary. New York: Oxford University Press, 1980.

American Heritage, Second College

The American Heritage Dictionary, second college edition. Boston: Houghton Mifflin Company, 1985. (First published in 1982.)

Webster's Ninth

Webster's Ninth New Collegiate Dictionary. Springfield: Merriam-Webster Inc., 1985. (First published in 1983.)

The Random House Dictionary of the English Language, classic edition. New
    York: Random House, 1983.

Webster's New Twentieth Century

Webster's New Twentieth Century Dictionary, second edition, unabridged.
    New York: Simon & Schuster, 1983.

Webster's New World

Webster's New World Dictionary, second college edition. New York: Simon
    & Schuster, 1984.

Webster's New World Guide

Chisholm, William S., Jr. *Webster's New World Guide to Pronunciation.* New
    York: Simon & Schuster, 1984.

NBC Handbook

Ehrlich, Eugene, and Raymond Hand, Jr. *NBC Handbook of Pronunciation,*
    fourth edition. New York: Harper & Row, 1984.

Webster's II New Riverside Dictionary. New York: Berkeley Books, 1984.

Everyday Reader's

Urdang, Laurence, ed. *The New York Times Everyday Reader's Dictionary of
    Misunderstood, Misused, and Mispronounced Words,* revised edition.
    New York: New American Library, 1985.

Random House II

The Random House Dictionary of the English Language, second edition, un-
    abridged. New York: Random House, 1987.

THE GUIDE

A

aberrant a-BER-ant or uh-BER-ant. *— adj. — deviating from what is normal*

Stress the second syllable (-ber-), in which the E has the sound of the E in BET or BERRY.

The word is now often pronounced AB-ur-ant. Only a handful of current dictionaries bother to list this rather recent, a-BER-ant pronunciation.

abyss uh-BIS, not AB-is. *— Noun — a bottomless pit*

academia AK-uh-**DEE**-mee-uh. *— Noun — the academic world*

This word is often mispronounced AK-uh-**DAY**-mee-uh.

accent AK-sent (noun); ak-SENT (verb). *— given 2nd choice in dictionary*

Properly, the AK-sent should fall on the second syllable of the verb to ak-SENT. See **decrease**.

accessory ak-SES-uh-ree, not uh-SES-uh-ree. See **flaccid**.

---

a = at • a̱ = woman • ah = spa • ahr = car • air = fair • ay = hay •
aw = saw • ch = chip • e = let • e̱ = item • ee = see • eer = deer
• i = sit • i̱ = direct • ng = sing • o̱ = connect • oh = go • oo =
soon • or = for • oor = poor • ow = cow • oy = toy • sh = she •
th = thin • t̲h̲ = them • u̱ = focus • uh = up • ur = turn • uu =
pull, took • y, eye = by, pie • zh = measure

acclimate uh-KLY-mit. Now usually AK-luh-mayt.

This word came into the language in 1792, and for well over a hundred years was pronounced uh-KLY-mit. This is the only pronunciation listed in Worcester (1884), *Century* (1914), *Webster's Collegiate* (1917), *New Century* (1927), and the *OED* (completed in 1928).

In 1926, W. H. P. Phyfe, in his *18,000 Words Often Mispronounced,* called the pronunciation AK-luh-mayt "a very frequent error." In 1934, *Webster* 2 legitimized AK-luh-mayt by listing it as an alternative pronunciation. For the next forty years dictionaries included AK-luh-mayt but continued to prefer uh-KLY-mit.

Of thirteen current authorities consulted, six prefer AK-luh-mayt, five prefer uh-KLY-mit, one gives only AK-luh-mayt, and one gives only uh-KLY-mit. Decide for yourself which has the stronger tradition. AK-luh-mayt may be destined to prevail, but until the last dictionary gives up on uh-KLY-mit, I will prefer it.

accompanist uh-KUHM-pa-nist, not uh-KUHM-pa-nee-ist.

accouterment uh-KOO-tur-ment, not uh-KOO-truh-ment.

It is the third syllable of this word (-ter-/-tre-) that causes all the trouble. *Accouterment* is so often spelled *accoutrement* (which some dictionaries prefer and others call "chiefly British") that many people now pronounce the word uh-KOO-truh-ment. No matter which spelling you prefer, the overwhelming number of authorities prefer that you say uh-KOO-tur-ment. If you are still not convinced, consider this: No one says THEE-uh-truh for *theatre,* SEN-truh for *centre,* MEE-gruh for *meagre,* or MY-truh for *mitre* when these words are spelled with the R before the E. Why should *accouterment* be an exception? Also, do not Gallicize the final syllable (-ment) by pronouncing it like MAW; this borrowing from a foreign tongue is not supported in English-language dictionaries.

accurate AK-yoor-it. Do not say AK-ur-it.

acumen uh-KYOO-men, not AK-yoo-men.

The accent is properly on the second syllable.

Although AK-yoo-men is gaining ground, only one authority prefers it—*Everyday Reader's Dictionary* (1985)—and only about half of my current sources include it.

adjective AJ-ik-tiv. AJ-uh-tiv is nonstandard. — *study this'*

A voice talent I once worked with told me an English teacher had taught her that AJ-ik-tiv, with the hard C audible (a hard C is pronounced like K), was wrong. That teacher probably also believed that you should never end a sentence with a preposition.

Sorry to be the teacher's pest, but the buck stops here. Only one source—*Webster's Ninth* (1985)—recognizes AJ-uh-tiv (it does not prefer it), and any reliable usage manual will tell you that there is nothing inherently wrong with ending a sentence with a preposition.

Adjectival, the corresponding AJ-ik-tiv, is pronounced AJ-ik-**TYV**-uul.

admirable AD-mi-ra-buul, not ad-MYR-uh-buul.

advertisement ad-vur-TYZ-ment.

The pronunciation ad-VUR-tiz-ment, with the accent on the second syllable (-ver-), is British, but was once preferred by many American dictionaries. It is now much less often heard in the United States, and for the last forty years the preferred American pronunciation has been ad-vur-TYZ-ment, with the accent on the third syllable, -tise.

aegis EE-jis. Do not say AY-jis. See **algae**.

aerie AIR-ee (like the adjective *airy*).

There are three alternative pronunciations for this word: EER-ee, AR-ee, and AY-uh-ree, which will be discussed below. First, the preferred pronunciation.

AIR-ee is the preference of the majority of sources past and present, from the *Century* (1914) and the *OED* (1928) to the *NBC Handbook* (1984), *Webster's New World* (1984), and *Random House II* (1987). AIR-ee has prevailed probably because of its similarity to such words as *aerial, aerate, aerobic,* etc., in which the Latin combining form AER-, air, is commonly pronounced AIR. This is fortuitous, however, for *aerie,* a nest in a high place, does not contain AER-, but comes from Middle English and Old French words meaning nest, and may be originally from the Latin *ager,* field.

EER-ee (EER- as in *beer*) has been listed in most dictionaries since the early part of the century but is almost never preferred. It may be a vestigial pronunciation based on the alternative spelling *eyrie,* popular in the eighteenth and nineteenth centuries, or perhaps it came about from the notion that the initial *ae-* is the Latin ligature, which is pronounced like long E (EE) in such words as *aeon,* the obsolescent spelling of *eon*; *Aeolian* (ee-OH-lee-in); and *aegis* (EE-jis).

AR-ee (A as in AT), which appeared about 1940, is included in some current dictionaries but is preferred only by *Webster's Ninth* (1985). It is probably chiefly a Northern and Midland regional pronunciation.

Finally, the tri-syllabic AY-ur-ee (AY- as in *day*) is the traditional pronunciation, preferred by nineteenth-century dictionaries as well as *Funk & Wagnalls New Standard* (1931) and *Webster 2* (1934). It is based on the older pronunciation of AER- in such words as *aerial* (formerly ay-EE-ree-al, now AIR-ee-al) and *aeronautics* (formerly AY-uh-ro-**NAW**-tiks, now AIR-uh-**NAW**-tiks), both from the

Latin AER, in which the vowels are pronounced separately: AH-air. It may also have been associated with similar words in which adjacent vowels were distinguished in pronunciation, e.g. *diaper* (DY-uh-pur) and *vacuum* (VAK-yoo-uhm). Some speakers still make this distinction (my mother does, of course), but today most blend these vowels into a digraph: *diaper* (DY-pur), *vacuum* (VAK-yoom), *aerie* (AIR-ee).

Aesop EE-s<u>u</u>p or EE-sahp.

The name of the famed writer of fables is often pronounced AY-sahp (AY- as in *day*), for which there is no authority. See **algae.**

affluence AF-loo-ints. Do not say uh-FLOO-ints.

Uh-FLOO-ints is a vogue pronunciation (see Appendix), which has only recently found its way into certain dictionaries. It is a shibboleth for those members of society who, by affecting what they imagine to be the superior practice of the gentry, would have others believe they are better, or better off. See **influence.**

algae AL-jee. Do not say AL-jay or AL-jy.

The ligature Æ, in words from Latin or Greek, is pronounced with a long E (EE as in NEED), especially when stressed. See **aegis**, **Aesop**, **alumnae**, **antennae**, **vertebrae**.

---

a = at • <u>a</u> = woman • ah = spa • ahr = car • air = fair • ay = hay • aw = saw • ch = chip • e = let • <u>e</u> = item • ee = see • eer = deer • i = sit • <u>i</u> = direct • ng = sing • <u>o</u> = connect • oh = go • oo = soon • or = for • oor = poor • ow = cow • oy = toy • sh = she • th = thin • <u>th</u> = them • <u>u</u> = focus • uh = up • ur = turn • uu = pull, took • y, eye = by, pie • zh = measure

---

alleged uh-LEJD.

The word should be pronounced in *two* syllables. The three-syllable pronunciation uh-LEJ-id is recognized by most current authorities, but is not preferred. See **supposed.**

alms AHMZ. Do not say AHLMZ. The L is silent. See **calm.**

alumnae uh-LUM-nee.

Alumnae is the Latin feminine plural of *alumna* (uh-LUM-nuh), a female graduate. The word is often mispronounced uh-LUM-ny (-ny as in *night*), which is the proper pronunciation for *alumni,* the Latin masculine plural of *alumnus* (uh-LUM-nuhs). *Alumni* can mean male graduates, or male and female graduates. *Alumnae* (uh-LUM-nee) refers only to female graduates. See **algae.**

amateur AM-uh-tur.

The pronunciation of this word has been a subject of controversy for many years. Should it be AM-uh-chur, AM-uh-toor, AM-uh-tyoor, or AM-uh-tur? In fact, all of these and even more variants are well established in the dictionaries, which differ considerably in their preferences. AM-uh-chur is probably now most often heard and preferred, and you will have plenty of good company if you say it this way; however, for some reason it also seems to be the pronunciation most criticized by those who choose not to use it. Therefore I recommend AM-uh-tur here in the belief that it is least likely to raise eyebrows, cause dyspepsia, or induce sneers.

ambergris AM-bur-grees, not AM-bur-gris.

The word should be pronounced like *amber* + *grease*. At least two current dictionaries prefer the pronunciation AM-bur-gris (-gris as in *gristle*), which apparently was not recorded in a dictionary until the 1930s. Most authorities, however, still prefer AM-bur-grees. The word comes from *amber* and the French *gris* (pronounced GREE), gray.

amenable un-MEE-na-buul.

The second syllable (-me) is pronounced like the word *me*.

The alternative pronunciation uh-MEN-a-buul, which perhaps arose because of its similarity to the word *amend,* has existed for at least seventy-five years. However, not one authority prefers it. Use uh-MEE-na-buul.

ancillary AN-si-ler-ee.

This is the standard American pronunciation. An-SIL-uh-ree, with the accent on the second syllable, is British.

antennae an-TEN-ee. Do not say an-TEN-eye. See **algae.**

apartheid a-PAHRT-hayt or a-PAHRT-hyt.

Apartheid came into the language in 1947 and hasn't stopped causing trouble since. Of thirteen recent dictionaries and pronunciation guides surveyed, six prefer a-PAHRT-hyt, four prefer a-PAHRT-hayt, and three prefer a-PAHR-tayt. I would prefer that we settle the issue once and for all, but that is as likely to happen as a speedy resolution to the political strife that spawned the word.

I have chosen to say a-PAHRT-hayt for the following reasons: The pronunciations a-PAHRT-hayt and a-PAHR-tayt are so close as to be nearly indistinguishable, and seven out of the thirteen sources I polled prefer one or the other. Also, to pronounce the word as though it were a combination of *apart* and *hate* seems to me an apt expression of both its meaning and its horrifying reality.

Never say a-PAHR-thyd. This common and particularly ugly spelling pronunciation (see Appendix) is not recognized by any authority I have consulted.

aphrodisiac af-roh-DIZ-ee-ak (DIZ-ee like *dizzy*).

The variant pronunciation af-roh-DEE-zee-ak is now often heard, and its popularity has persuaded the editors of *Random House II* (1987) and *Webster's Ninth* (1985) to give it precedence. All of my other sources, however, give only af-roh-DIZ-ee-ak.

apparatus Properly, ap-uh-RAY-tus, not ap-uh-RAT-us. See **data.**

applicable AP-li-kuh-buul, not uh-PLIK-uh-buul.

The accent should be on AP-, the first syllable. The pronunciation uh-PLIK-uh-buul, with the stress on the second syllable, has existed for at least forty years, but no authority prefers it. See **despicable**, **explicable**, **exquisite**, **hospitable**, **lamentable**, **summarily**.

apricot AY-pri-kaht or AP-ri-kaht.

Dictionaries preferred the long A (AY-pri-kaht) until about 1970, when they began a gradual shift over to the short A (AP-ri-kaht), which is now generally preferred. In fact, *Random House II* (1987) has taken the liberty of altering the way the word has always been divided, changing it from the traditional *a-pri-cot* to *ap-ri-cot,* probably to reflect the current preference in pronunciation.

I grew up hearing and saying AP-ri-kaht, but was surprised to discover that hardly anyone I encountered outside my region (New York City and New England) pronounced it this way. Whether you say AY-pri-kaht or AP-ri-kaht, you will not be wrong. However, on account if its longer tradition in the dictionaries (and because I love to protract a controversy about words), I recommend AY-pri-kaht.

aqua- AK-w<u>a</u>, not AHK-w<u>a</u>.

The authorities are in agreement that the initial A in this combining form should have the sound of the A in *cat,* not the sound of the A in *father.* This preference governs the proper pronunciation of *aquamarine* (AK-w<u>a</u>-m<u>a</u>-reen); *aquatint* (AK-w<u>a</u>-tint); *aquaplane* (AK-w<u>a</u>-playn); and nearly all other words beginning with *aqua-* where the stress falls on the first syllable, including *aqueduct,* which is spelled differently but pronounced AK-w<u>a</u>-duhkt (not AH-kw<u>a</u>-duhkt).

aqueous AY-kwee-<u>us</u> (AY- as in *day*), not AK-wee-<u>us</u>.

This word is the exception to the rule outlined under **aqua-**. Unlike the examples given there, in which the first syllable is *aq-* (pronounced AK), the first syllable of *aqueous* is a solitary *a-* (*a-que-ous*), and so is pronounced like A in *hay*. The alternative pronunciation AK-wee-<u>us</u> has been listed by most dictionaries for about fifty years, but is not preferred.

archaeology AHR-kee-**AHL**-uh-jee, not AHR-kay-**AHL**-uh-jee.

The second syllable (-chae-) should be pronounced like the word *key,* not like the name *Kay*.

archangel AHRK-ayn-juul.

---

a = at • <u>a</u> = woman • ah = spa • ahr = car • air = fair • ay = hay • aw = saw • ch = chip • e = let • <u>e</u> = item • ee = see • eer = deer • i = sit • <u>i</u> = direct • ng = sing • <u>o</u> = connect • oh = go • oo = soon • or = for • oor = poor • ow = cow • oy = toy • sh = she • th = thin • <u>th</u> = them • <u>u</u> = focus • uh = up • ur = turn • uu = pull, took • y, eye = by, pie • zh = measure

archetype AHRK-i̲-typ. Do not say ARCH-i̲-typ.

The adjective *archetypal* may be pronounced AHR-ki̲-**TYP**-uul or **AHRK**-i̲-TYP-uul, with the accent on either the third or the first syllable.

arctic AHRK-tik. Do not say AHR-tik.

This word is almost universally mispronounced. Take care also with the adjective *antarctic* (ant-AHRK-tik, *not* ant-AHR-tik, or even worse, an-AHR-tik) and the continent *Antarctica* (ant-AHRK-ti-ka̲). Be sure to articulate the hard C (pronounced like K) in the *arc-* of all these words.

argot AHR-goh or AHR-gu̲t.

Argot, which came into English in 1860 from French, by derivation refers specifically to the secret language of beggars, tramps, or thieves. In this century it has come to be used more generally to mean jargon, specialized vocabulary.

The pronunciation AHR-goh is closer to the French, and AHR-gu̲t is anglicized—more English. Since about 1900, most dictionaries have given both, with AHR-goh first. (See *Or* in the Appendix.)

asbestos as-BES-to̲s or az-BES-to̲s.

The last syllable (-tos) is the one to watch out for in this word. *Asbestos* is often mispronounced as-BES-tohs or az-BES-tohs. The last syllable should rhyme with *us* or *kiss,* not with *dose.* (Though rarely used, the alternative spelling *asbestus,* with a final -tus instead of -tos, better indicates the proper pronunciation of the word.)

Asbestosis, the disease caused by inhaling asbestos, is pronounced AS-bes-**TOH**-sis or AZ-bes-**TOH**-sis.

assembly uh-SEM-blee, not uh-SEM-buh-lee, which adds an extra syllable to the word.

assuage uh-SWAYJ, not uh-SWAYZH, uh-SWAHZH, or uh-SWAHJ.

This is the story of how a decade or two of neglect can ruin what has been established for centuries. *Assuage* has been in the language for seven hundred years, and since dictionaries began giving pronunciation there has been only one way to say the word: uh-SWAYJ. In the last three years, however, two dictionaries have recognized the variant pronunciations uh-SWAYZH and uh-SWAHZH.

Modern dictionaries must serve two masters: They must show us what is accepted or traditional in language, and therefore considered correct; and they must record what is going on in language—the changes and trends—right or wrong, good or bad. Thus, if a word that has been pronounced or used in one way for seven hundred years suddenly is pronounced or used in a new way by many people, dictionary makers are compelled to record that fact.

This is the proper function of a dictionary. The proper function of this book, however, is to advise and prescribe. *Assuage* has always been pronounced uh-SWAYJ, and there is no good reason why we should not continue to say it that way.

The question remains: After so many centuries of calm agreement, who is rocking the boat, and why? Those who now mispronounce *assuage* very likely have read widely and command a large vocabulary, for this is not the sort of word you encounter every day in the newspaper or on television. Apparently, though, they have never heard it pronounced correctly, nor have they checked the pronunciation as well as the definition. Chances are they simply guessed how it should be pronounced.

athlete ATH-leet.

Do not say ATH-uh-leet. This is a very common error, especially among *athletes* themselves, as well as among sportscasters, who should know better. Don't pick up their bad habit. There is no vowel between the H and the L in this word, and no justification for adding a syllable to it.

atmospheric at-muhs-FER-ik. Regionally, at-muhs-FAIR-ik.

The *pher-* in *atmospheric* should be pronounced like *fer-* in *ferry,* not like the word *fear.* It may help to remember that *pheric* is always pronounced like the word *ferric* (FER-ik), which means of or containing iron.

Do not say at-mos-FEER-ik. The word has so often been mispronounced this way that a few current sources now prefer this pronunciation. The majority, however, do not. See **hysteria**, **schizophrenia**, **spherical**.

auxiliary awg-ZIL-yuh-ree. Do not say awg-ZIL-uh-ree.

Be sure to articulate the Y sound in the third syllable.

The mispronunciation awg-ZIL-uh-ree is so common that it is now given as a variant in most current dictionaries. However, *auxiliary* is one of a number of words that many people have singled out as a way of judging how well you speak. If you say awg-ZIL-uh-ree you may be criticized for it, but no one can fault you for saying awg-ZIL-yuh-ree. See **accurate**, **arctic**, **athlete**, **height**, **heinous**, **jewelry**, **mischievous**, **nuclear**, **often**, **wash**.

B

bacchanal bak-uh-NAL or BAK-uh-nuul.

Until the 1960s, dictionaries recorded only one pronunciation for this word: BAK-uh-nuul (BAK- like *back,* -nuul rhyming with *full*). Since then variants have proliferated, of which the most frequently recorded are bak-uh-NAL (-NAL rhyming with *pal*) and bah-kuh-NAHL (with the A in bah- and -NAHL like the A in *father*). Both shift the accent from the first to the third syllable.

Random House II (1987) prefers bah-kuh-NAHL. However, *Webster's Ninth* (1985) and *Webster's New World* (1984) still list BAK-uh-nuul first, and bak-uh-NAL is preferred by the *American Heritage,* Second College (1985); the *NBC Handbook* (1984); *Webster's New World Guide* (1984); and other current sources. See **bacchus**.

bacchus BAK-us, not BAH-kus. See **bacchanal**.

---

a = at • a̲ = woman • ah = spa • ahr = car • air = fair • ay = hay •
aw = saw • ch = chip • e = let • e̲ = item • ee = see • eer = deer
• i = sit • i̲ = direct • ng = sing • o̲ = connect • oh = go • oo =
soon • or = for • oor = poor • ow = cow • oy = toy • sh = she •
th = thin • t̲h̲ = them • u̲ = focus • uh = up • ur = turn • uu =
pull, took • y, eye = by, pie • zh = measure

bade BAD. Do not say BAYD.

This word should rhyme with *sad*, not with *aid*.

Bade is the past tense and past participle of the verb to *bid*. Some dictionaries now recognize the spelling pronunciation BAYD, but not one prefers it. See **forbade**.

balk BAWK. Do not say BAWLK.

The L is silent, as in *talk* and *walk*.

balm BAHM. Do not pronounce the L.

This word is pronounced like *bomb*. See **calm**.

banal BAY-nal. Also buh-NAL.

This is a word of many pronunciations, each of which has its outspoken and intractable proponents. Though it may pain some to hear it, let the record show that BAY-nal is the one preferred by the overwhelming number of authorities of the last century. Advocates for BAY-nal include Worcester (1884); the *OED* (1928); *Webster* 2 (1934); *Webster* 3 (1961); three Funk & Wagnalls dictionaries (1931, 1962, and 1980); and *Webster's New World* (1984).

The pronunciation buh-NAL (which rhymes with *canal*) is also acceptable. It is listed second (usually after BAY-nal) by many authorities and is preferred by *Webster's Ninth* (1985) and *Random House II* (1987).

The pronunciation buh-NAHL (where the second syllable rhymes with *doll*) is preferred by the Boston-based Houghton Mifflin lexicographers (purveyors of the *American Heritage* dictionaries) and by the *NBC Handbook* (1984).

The pronunciation BAN-ul (which rhymes with *channel*) is the preference of a number of older authorities, most notably the *Century* (1914) and *New Century* (1927). It rarely appears in recent dictionaries.

barbiturate bar-BICH-ur-it.

Many speakers fail to articulate the R in the last syllable of this word. Be careful to say barbitu*r*ate. Do not say bar-BICH-oo-it.

Barbiturate came into the language in the late 1920s. There were two original pronunciations: bar-buh-TYOOR-it, with the accent on the third syllable to make it analogous with its source, *barbituric* (bar-buh-TYOOR-ik), the adjective pertaining to the acid of that name; and bar-BICH-uh-rayt, with the accent on the second syllable and the final syllable pronounced like *rate*. Both of these are still listed in most current dictionaries, though they are now heard infrequently.

basal BAY-s<u>a</u>l, not BAY-z<u>a</u>l.

basil BAZ-<u>i</u>l. (BAZ- rhymes with *has.*)

BAZ-<u>i</u>l is the preferred pronunciation for the herb, the name (Basil), the sheepskin tanned with bark, and the ankle iron or fetter for a prisoner.

Webster 3 (1961) is the first of my sources to recognize variants, listing BAY-s<u>i</u>l, BAS-<u>i</u>l, and BAY-z<u>i</u>l. Of these, the last is now most often given as an alternative, but only one source, *Webster's New World Guide* (1984), puts it first. Thirty years of saying BAY-z<u>i</u>l hardly seems enough to justify granting it—or any other way of saying the word—precedence over BAZ-<u>i</u>l, which was the only recognized pronunciation until the middle of this century.

behemoth bi-HEE-m<u>u</u>th.

In the nineteenth century, this word was pronounced with the accent on the first syllable: BEE-huh-mawth or BEE-uh-m<u>u</u>th. This is the preference of Worcester (1884) and *Webster's International* (1890), also known as "Old Webster." By the 1930s, however, the tide had turned, with the *Century* (1914), the *OED* (1928), and *Webster* 2 (1934) rallying behind bi-HEE-muth, and later dictionaries following suit. The former pronunciation is still listed in most current sources, but *Webster's New World Guide* (1984) points out that it has become rare.

beneficent buh-NEF-i-sent.

Be careful with the second syllable (-nef-). Do not say buh-NIF-i-sent.

benignant buh-NIG-nant. Do not say buh-NY-nant.

Benign (buh-NYN) and *benignant* follow the pronunciation of *malign* (muh-LYN) and *malignant* (muh-LIG-nant).

bequeath be-KWEETH.

The TH should sound like the TH in *this* and *bathe,* not like the TH in *thin* and *path.* Also, do not pronounce the first syllable like the verb *be;* because *be-* is unstressed, the E is lightened so that the syllable sounds like BI or BUH.

bestial BES-chuul or BEST-yuul. BES-tee-uul is British.

Since the 1960s, dictionaries have given BEES-chuul as an alternative because many people had mistakenly begun to model their pronunciation of *bestial* after the word *beast.*

Dictionaries are too egalitarian to tell you why they don't prefer BEES-chuul, but for your protection, I will: It is considered by careful speakers to be a truly beastly pronunciation. Why? For the arbitrary reason that it separates those who pay attention to propriety in speech from those who do not. That may seem ridiculous, but all custom is ridiculous in a way. The pronunciation of this word is a matter of etiquette or a mark of refinement, like handling your silverware properly or covering your mouth when you cough. If that sort of thing matters to you when it comes to speech then you should know that BES-chuul is the *best* pronunciation, and BEES-chuul is *beast*ly.

bestiality BES-chee-**AL**-i-tee, not BEES-chee-**AL**-i-tee. See **bestial**.

blithe BLY<u>TH</u> (rhymes with *writhe*).

How do you pronounce the title of Noel Coward's play *Blithe Spirit*? Does the TH of *blithe* sound like the TH in *then* or in *thin*? You may have heard many speakers say BLYTH, with the TH of *thin*, but the correct pronunciation is BLY<u>TH</u>, with the TH of *then*. Here's why:

When a monosyllabic word ends in *-the*, the TH is usually sounded or "voiced," as in *clothe, breathe,* and *soothe*. When the TH is final, it is usually "voiceless," as in *cloth, breath,* and *forsooth. Blithe* follows this rule, and so is pronounced with the TH of *then* and *there,* not with the TH of *path*.

Since 1961, when *Webster* 3 appeared, Merriam-Webster's dictionaries have preferred the pronunciation BLYTH (TH as in *thin*) over BLYTH (TH as in *then*). If a recent Merriam-Webster is the only dictionary you own, you should know that their opinion is an anomaly: No other authority in the last century prefers BLYTH (TH as in *thin*), and Merriam-Webster's previous unabridged dictionary— *Webster* 2 (1934)—gives only BLY<u>TH</u>. See **lithe**, **loath**, **loathsome**.

---

a = at • a̱ = woman • ah = spa • ahr = car • air = fair • ay = hay • aw = saw • ch = chip • e = let • e̱ = item • ee = see • eer = deer • i = sit • i̱ = direct • ng = sing • o̱ = connect • oh = go • oo = soon • or = for • oor = poor • ow = cow • oy = toy • sh = she • th = thin • t̲h̲ = them • u̱ = focus • uh = up • ur = turn • uu = pull, took • y, eye = by, pie • zh = measure

bolivar boh-LEE-vahr.

I recommend this one pronunciation for both the monetary unit of Venezuela and the name of the nineteenth-century South American liberator. It is a personal preference, based on the following assumptions:

1. There seems to me to be a general trend among educated speakers and the broadcast media to pronounce foreign names in the way they are pronounced in the language they come from. In cases where that would cause spasms in the English-speaking tongue, we try to come as close as possible to the original without mangling the name or the organ of speech.

2. It is your inalienable right to demand that your name be pronounced the way you want it to be pronounced. Unfortunately, this right is not very often respected, especially with celebrities and historical figures (see **Carnegie**). Since Mr. Bolívar is not here to plead his case, I will have to do it for him. In Spanish as well as in English orthography, there is an accent mark over the I in the name Bolívar. It is not there for embellishment; that is where the stress falls. There is also an accent mark in the man's first name, Simón. The entire Spanish-speaking world calls him Simón (see-MOHN) Bolívar (boh-LEE-vahr). Since that is quite pronounceable by English speakers I see no reason why we shouldn't do the same.

3. Finally, the name of the unit of currency comes from the name of the historical figure. Therefore, using the same pronunciation for both is sensible, consistent, and simplifies things considerably.

For the plural of the monetary unit, I recommend the spelling *bolivars* and the pronunciation boh-LEE-vahrz.

bouquet boo-KAY (boo- as in *boot*) or boh-KAY (boh- as in *boat*).

Older dictionaries prefer boo-KAY; some do not even list boh-KAY. However, since about the 1950s most dictionaries have preferred boh-KAY, except when the word is used to mean an aroma, as "The [boo-KAY] of this wine." Why such a distinction is necessary is beyond me. Maybe it came about because the connoisseurs all stuck to boo-KAY after hoi polloi had cast their ballots for boh-KAY. Now I suppose we'll have to say, "The [boo-KAY] of your [boh-KAY] is mighty fine, ma'am." Frankly, that smells a bit fishy to me, but *de gustibus non est disputandum*. Take your pick—but remember, the accent must be on the second syllable. I'm sticking with the perennial boo-KAY.

boudoir BOO-dwahr, not BUU-dwahr.

The first syllable (bou-) rhymes with *too*. Most dictionaries prefer the stress on the first syllable, but stressing the second (boo-DWAHR) is also acceptable.

Brobdingnagian BROB-ding-**NAG**-ee-in.

Be sure to pronounce the second syllable like the word *ding*. It is often mispronounced DIG, probably because the word is often misspelled *Brobdignagian*.

The word refers to the gigantic inhabitants of the imaginary land of Brobdingnag in Jonathan Swift's *Gulliver's Travels,* or to anyone or anything like them. It should be capitalized.

brooch BROHCH.

Properly, *brooch* should rhyme with *coach*. The pronunciation BROOCH, which rhymes with *smooch*, is usually listed but not preferred. Both pronunciations exist because, historically, *brooch,* an ornamental clasp, is the same word as *broach* (now usually used as a verb to mean to utter, introduce, or open for the first time), and most dictionaries still give the alternative spelling *broach* for *brooch*.

Though many speakers are still confused, the dictionaries judiciously settled the divorce of these two words a long time ago: Whether the word is spelled *brooch* or *broach,* and regardless of the meaning intended, the preferred pronunciation is BROHCH, rhyming with *coach*. See **joust**.

bulimia byoo-LIM-ee-uh.

Do not say boo-LEE-mee-uh or buh-LEE-mee-uh. These are recent and now very common mispronunciations.

Bulimia came into the language in the fourteenth century, and until 1987 the only recognized pronunciation was byoo-LIM-ee-uh. In the last ten or fifteen years the word has leapt from medical manuals into the vernacular, and in response to widespread confusion over how it is pronounced, *Random House II* (1987) has dutifully recorded the following variants: byoo-LEE-mee-uh, boo-LIM-ee-uh, boo-LEE-mee-uh, buh-LIM-ee-uh, and buh-LEE-mee-uh. Is the word really so hard to pronounce properly? Why didn't the newscasters and TV "Movie of the Week" directors check the *NBC Handbook* before going on the air? In the rush to be trendy, didn't anyone bother to look it up?

I try to be fair-minded, so I'll admit that boo- instead of byoo- for the first syllable is acceptable, and if you push me I'll even grant you buh-. But LEE-mee-uh instead of LIM-ee-uh for the rest is outrageous. It's like saying LEE-muh-zeen for *limousine* or LEE-mur-ik for *limerick*. There's got to be a LEE-mit to this sort of thing.

Boulimia, a nineteenth-century variant spelling of the word, apparently still occurs often enough to warrant inclusion in *Random House II*. It seems unlikely, however, that it would have influenced the current mispronunciation of the word. It is interesting to note, though, that the oldest form of the word is *bulimy,* for which dictionaries have always given the pronunciation BYOO-li-mee.

It may be a little disconcerting at first to be the only

one in the neighborhood who says byoo-LIM-ee-uh, but I guarantee you'll get used to it. You will also be *right*.

Byzantine BIZ-in-teen or BIZ-in-tyn or bi-ZAN-tin.

This is one of those words that reveals how old you are, how old your dictionary is, or both. Orthoepic carbon-dating has shown that BIZ-in-tin (not listed above) is preferred by people as old as ancient Greece; bi-ZAN-tin is preferred by people as old as the hills; BIZ-in-tyn is preferred by people old enough to get away with trying to sound British by making the I in the last syllable long; BIZ-in-teen (which rose to prominence between the Great Depression and the McCarthy era) is now preferred by most, even those who can remember the good old days; and BY-zin-teen, BY-zin-tyn, BY-zin-tin, and several other variations also not listed above are the choices of a small, select group of eccentrics entirely out of touch with reality.

I choose to say bi-ZAN-tin partly because my favorite American dictionaries prefer it (how's that for an arbitrary reason?), and you will still find it listed in most dictionaries today.* It also strikes me as the most sensible of all the

---

*For various reasons, which extend beyond the treatment of pronunciation, my favorite dictionaries are: the *Century* (1889–1914) and *Webster* 2 (1934). Other sources preferring bi-ZAN-tin include Phyfe (1926); Kenyon and Knott (1949); *Funk & Wagnalls New Standard* (1931); *Funk & Wagnalls New Practical Standard* (1962); and *Webster's New Twentieth Century,* second edition (1983).

---

a = at • a̱ = woman • ah = spa • ahr = car • air = fair • ay = hay • aw = saw • ch = chip • e = let • e̱ = item • ee = see • eer = deer • i = sit • i̱ = direct • ng = sing • o̱ = connect • oh = go • oo = soon • or = for • oor = poor • ow = cow • oy = toy • sh = she • th = thin • t̲h̲ = them • u̱ = focus • uh = up • ur = turn • uu = pull, took • y, eye = by, pie • zh = measure

possibilities because it retains the accent of the place it refers to, Byzantium—which, thankfully, all sources agree is properly pronounced bi-ZAN-shee-<u>um</u>, with the accent on the second syllable (-zan-) and the TI pronounced SHEE, as in *consortium*. See **consortium**.

C

cadre KAD-ree or KAH-dur.

Cadre is a good example of how words taken directly from other languages become anglicized, gradually become more English in their pronunciation and usage.

All sources agree that the word comes from the French *cadre,* which in turn comes from the Latin *quadrum,* but there seems to be some disagreement over when it entered English. *Random House II* places its entry between 1905 and 1910. *Cadre* appears, however, in Worcester (1884), and the *OED* cites examples of its use in print from 1830 through 1870. (I guess it must have been a rough night in bad light when the editors at Random House wrote the etymology for *cadre.*)

Until the 1950s, dictionaries preferred the pronunciation KAH-dur, after the French, or sometimes KAD-ur, with an anglicized A (as in *hat*). Around the middle of the century, dictionaries began to record another pronunciation, common among the military: KAD-ree.

It is usual for a word to become fully anglicized in pronunciation within fifty to a hundred years, though nowadays this time is shrinking. This tendency, which was probably hastened by the fact that *cadre* is chiefly a military term, caused speakers to abandon the French-sounding KAH-dur and adopt the anglicized KAD-ree.

In 1961, *Webster* 3 gave precedence to KAD-ree, and since then authorities have continued to prefer it. However, another variant, KAH-dray (which has also existed since the 1960s), has grown in popularity enough to be listed second in several current dictionaries.

KAH-dray is a de-anglicized pronunciation, an attempt to return to what speakers think is the original, or foreign, pronunciation of the word. It is not the original English pronunciation, though, and it makes the word sound as if it comes from Italian or Spanish rather than French. If a word has gone through the full process of anglicization there is no reason to return halfway; if we return at all it should be the whole nine yards. To say KAH-dur, which is closest to the French, makes more sense than saying KAH-dray, which is neither French nor English. To say KAD-ree may not sound pretty, but it is definitely English. See **foyer**, **junta**, **largess**, **lingerie**.

calm KAHM.

Calm rhymes with *bomb*. The pronunciation KAHLM, which has been around for about thirty years, is recognized in some dictionaries but not preferred. In *calm, palm, balm, qualm, psalm,* and *alms* (and in *balk, talk, walk, caulk, chalk,* and *stalk*) the L should be silent. (See Spelling Pronunciation in the Appendix.)

capricious kuh-PRISH-us, not kuh-PREE-shus.

The second syllable should rhyme with WISH, not with WE.

Kuh-PREE-shus, a spelling pronunciation (see Appendix) based on the word *caprice* (kuh-PREES), was first recognized in the 1960s. It is now listed as an alternative in some dictionaries, but is not preferred. See **prestigious**.

caramel KA-ruh-muul. Regionally, KAHR-muul.

The pronunciation KA-ruh-muul (KA-ruh- as in *carrot,* -muul rhyming with *pull*) is preferred by all authorities, past and present. In the 1940s and 1950s, dictionaries began to list KAHR-muul (KAHR- like *car*) as a variant, but seemed insecure about its standing. Kenyon and Knott (1949) add the vague comment: "In many places [KAHR-muul] is often heard"; the *American College* (1953) says, "Midwest often KAHR-muul."

By 1961, KAHR-muul had acquired a bad rap. According to *Webster* 3, it was "unacceptable to many." *Webster* 3 listed another variant, KA-ruh-mel (-mel rhyming with *fell*), also classifying it as unacceptable.

Since then, KAHR-muul and KA-ruh-mel have risen from the gutter of descriptive lexicography into widespread acceptance, a sweet-toothed success story in which the influence of television's candy bar commercials cannot be overlooked. Today most dictionaries recognize KAHR-muul, the regional pronunciation, and KA-ruh-mel, the spelling pronunciation (see Appendix). However, the traditional and preferred pronunciation remains KA-ruh-muul.

Carnegie (Andrew) kahr-NAY-gee or kahr-NEG-ee.

"The accent is on the *second* syllable." —Andrew Carnegie.

Webster 2 (1934) says, "The pronunciation with ā [kahr-NAY-gee] was that of Mr. Carnegie himself, but as the

---

a = at • a̱ = woman • ah = spa • ahr = car • air = fair • ay = hay • aw = saw • ch = chip • e = let • e̱ = item • ee = see • eer = deer • i = sit • i̱ = direct • ng = sing • o̱ = connect • oh = go • oo = soon • or = for • oor = poor • ow = cow • oy = toy • sh = she • th = thin • t̲h̲ = them • u̱ = focus • uh = up • ur = turn • uu = pull, took • y, eye = by, pie • zh = measure

Scotch ā is 'stopped,' that is, pronounced with no terminal glide, it sounds like ĕ [kahr-NEG-ee] to many."

For the famous concert hall in New York City, general practice has followed regional preference in placing the accent on the first syllable, although some speakers (even in New York) still stress the second. For the renowned friend maker and people influencer, Dale Carnegie, the accent on the first syllable is also most commonly heard. See **bolivar**.

Caribbean ka-ri̱-BEE-a̱n.

The accent should be on the BE in *Caribbean*. The pronunciation kuh-RIB-ee-a̱n, with the accent on the second syllable, has been recorded in dictionaries since the 1930s but is not preferred.

caveat KAY-vee-at (KAY- as in *cave*, -at like *at*).

Until the 1960s, dictionaries gave no other pronunciation for this word. *Webster 3* (1961) is the first of my sources to record an alternative pronunciation: KAH-vee-aht. Since then variants have proliferated. We now have KAV-ee-aht (KAV- as in *caviar*), preferred by *Webster's Ninth* (1985) and *Random House II* (1987); KAV-ee-at, preferred by the *NBC Handbook;* KAH-vee-aht, listed by many but preferred by none; as well as variants in which the A in the final syllable (-at) is a schwa, in other words, pronounced like the A in *ago* or *final*.

In this mad market of possibilities, I say, *caveat emptor*—let the buyer beware. The pronunciation with the best warranty is KAY-vee-at. Its satisfied customers go back a hundred years or more, and it is still the trusted choice of many today, including *Webster's New World* (1984); *Funk & Wagnalls Standard* (1980); *Scribner–Bantam* (1979); *Everyday Reader's* (1985); and the New College (1982) and Second College (1985) editions of *American Heritage*.

celebratory SEL-e-bra-tor-ee. Also, suh-LEB-ra-tor-ee.

This word came into the language in 1926. Strange to say, it is hard to find in a dictionary. Only seven of my sources list it. Four mark it SEL-e-bra-tor-ee (the *OED*; *Webster* 3; *Funk & Wagnalls Standard*; and *Webster's Ninth*). Two mark it suh-LEB-ra-tor-ee (*Webster* 2 and *Webster's New World*). *Random House II* gives both pronunciations, with SEL-e-bra-tor-ee first. The odds clearly favor SEL-e-bra-tor-ee, but I find it hard to pass harsh judgment against suh-LEB-ra-tor-ee when two very fine dictionaries prefer it.

cerebral SER-uh-bral. Now often suh-REE-bral.

The pronunciation suh-REE-bral has been heard for about seventy-five years, but was not recognized by dictionaries until the 1940s or 1950s. The *American College* (1953) is the first of my sources to record it. In 1961, *Webster* 3 gave it precedence, and since then it has gained greatly in popularity.

Current dictionaries are about evenly divided. Analogy and past authority favor SER-uh-bral, so I recommend it, but suh-REE-bral is so prevalent that one cannot legitimately fault it.

chaise longue shayz-LAWNG.

This word comes directly from French and means literally "long chair." Note that the CH in *chaise* is pronounced like SH in *shade*. Do not say CHAYS (like *chase*).

So many speakers have mispronounced this word chays-LOWNJ that many dictionaries now list the alternative spelling *chaise lounge*. But the lexicographers aren't lounging around in their loafers, or loafing around on their lounges. When the word is spelled *chaise lounge,* they say you may pronounce *lounge* as LOWNJ, but you still have to say SHAYZ for *chaise*. The way I see it, you might as well spell it *chaise longue,* pronounce it shayz-LAWNG, and relax.

chassis SHAS-ee or CHAS-ee.

There is equal authority for both these pronunciations. SHAS-ee has been favored longer and has the edge in the number of sources that list it first, but CHAS-ee is preferred by many current authorities and may eventually prevail.

Dictionaries sometimes also give CHA-sis or SHA-sis, with the final S sounded. These occur infrequently, and should probably be avoided.

chemise shu-MEEZ.

The only source that lists an alternative pronunciation is *Webster's Ninth* (1985), which gives shu-MEES. Say shu-MEEZ.

chicanery shi-KAY-nur-ee, not chi-KAY-nur-ee.

Shi-KAY-nur-ee is the traditional and proper pronunciation. The variant chi-KAY-nur-ee is often listed in current dictionaries, but is not preferred.

Chicano chi-KAH-noh.

Do not say shi-KAH-noh or chi-KAN-oh (KAN like *can*). These are wrong. The pronunciation chee-KAH-noh, in which the I in the first syllable has a long E sound, as in *cheek,* is Spanish. It is preferred by many bilingual (English–Spanish) speakers, both Hispanic and non-Hispanic. The pronunciation chi-KAH-noh is appropriate in all English-language contexts.

chiropodist ky-RAHP-uh-dist or ki-RAHP-uh-dist.

The CH is pronounced like a K. Do not say shi-RAHP-uh-dist. Also, in careful speech the first syllable (chi-) should clearly rhyme with *high*. This is the marking of older sources, the preference of the *Everyday Reader's Dictionary* (1985), and the pronunciation used by many cultivated speakers today.

chivalrous SHIV-al-rus, not shi-VAL-rus.

SHIV-al-rus, with the accent on the first syllable, is the only pronunciation given in most dictionaries. This word's noble partner, *chivalric,* is another story, however. For the first half of this century, the pronunciations SHIV-al-rik and shi-VAL-rik coexisted, with some authorities preferring the former. But in the last thirty years the tide has turned, and all current authorities prefer shi-VAL-rik.

cliché klee-SHAY, not kli-SHAY.

Careful speakers preserve the KLEE (rhymes with *see*) sound of the first syllable. See **clique**.

clique KLEEK, not KLIK.

This word should rhyme with *seek,* not *slick.* See **cliché**.

coitus KOH-i-tus.

This word is very often mispronounced. The problem comes from not knowing where to put the stress, and those who shift it to the second syllable are then unsure how to pronounce the I. This insecurity can produce some astonishing results—I have heard koh-EYE-tus, koh-AY-tus, and COY-tus, all of which may be in the Kamasutra but are not, to my knowledge, in any dictionary. Several current authorities do recognize one alternative pronunciation, koh-EE-tus, but *Random House II* (1987) says there's only one way to do it, and that's KOH-i-tus.

---

a = at • a = woman • ah = spa • ahr = car • air = fair • ay = hay • aw = saw • ch = chip • e = let • e = item • ee = see • eer = deer • i = sit • i = direct • ng = sing • o = connect • oh = go • oo = soon • or = for • oor = poor • ow = cow • oy = toy • sh = she • th = thin • th = them • u = focus • uh = up • ur = turn • uu = pull, took • y, eye = by, pie • zh = measure

colander KUHL-an-dur, not KAHL-an-dur.

The first syllable (col-) rhymes with *dull*, not *doll*.

This word came into the language in 1450. Like many early English words, it was spelled in a variety of strange ways over the years. By the end of the nineteenth century the field had narrowed to two standard spellings: *colander* and *cullender*. After another half-century of duking it out, *colander* won the preferred spelling title, and *cullender* won second prize—pronunciation.

In a winner-takes-all society, however, the runner-up rarely gets any respect. As it became clear that *colander* had the edge in spelling (c. 1920–1930), many people started pronouncing it as it was spelled (see Spelling Pronunciation in the Appendix). But in reviewing the match, those great referees, the dictionaries, have continued to defend their original decision. Preferred spelling: *colander*. Preferred pronunciation: *cullender*. See **brooch**.

collate kuh-LAYT or kah-LAYT.

The first syllable of *collate* is unstressed, and therefore pronounced with a schwa or obscure vowel sound, as it is in similar words beginning with *coll-*: *collect, collide, collapse, collision, collaborate, collateral,* and so on. This is the preference of nearly all authorities, past and present.

Also acceptable, though not often preferred, is the pronunciation kah-LAYT. Here the first syllable (col-) is pronounced like the first syllable of *college,* but the stress remains on the second syllable (-late).

Other variants listed in most current dictionaries include koh-LAYT, KAH-layt, and KOH-layt. Only the *NBC Handbook* (1984) prefers koh-LAYT, only the *Oxford American* (1980) and *Webster's New World Guide* (1984) prefer KAH-layt, and KOH-layt, though now often heard, is not preferred by any of my sources.

collation kuh-LAY-shin or kah-LAY-shin.

Preference is about evenly divided between these two pronunciations for *collation,* which may mean either a light meal, snack, or the act or process of collating (kuh-LAY-ting). Avoid the pronunciation koh-LAY-shin, in which the first syllable has the long O of *cola.* It is listed by some current dictionaries but is not preferred. See **collate**.

combatant kom-BAT-int.

The pronunciation KAHM-buh-tint, once preferred by American dictionaries, is now chiefly British.

comparable KAHM-pur-uh-buul, not kuhm-PAIR-uh-buul.

The stress is properly on the first syllable—but watch out: Do not say KAHM-pruh-buul. *Comparable* should have four clearly articulated syllables: KAHM-pur-uh-buul. See **admirable**, **formidable**, **irreparable**, **reparable**.

conch KAHNGK, not KAHNCH.

Conch, a large, spiral seashell, should rhyme with *honk.* The plural is *conchs* (KAHNGKS) or *conches* (KAHN-chiz).

consortium kun-SOR-shee-um, not kun-SOR-tee-um.

Also, do not say kun-SOR-shum. The word should have four syllables.

The paramount issue here is whether the TI in *consortium* should be pronounced like SH in *sheep* or like the word *tea.* The answer is that to do the latter is to be guilty not only of spelling pronunciation (see Appendix) but also of vogue pronunciation. Vogue pronunciations —to borrow a phrase or two from H. W. Fowler—are "taken up merely as novel variants on their predecessors," often only for "the joy of showing that one has acquired them."

One unfortunate characteristic of vogue pronunciations is that they have a certain snob appeal that enables them to catch on very quickly and so get into the dictionaries. Three recent sources now prefer kun-SOR-tee-um; the rest, however, stand by kun-SOR-shee-um, with some not even listing the vogue pronunciation. (See the Appendix for more on Vogue Pronunciations.)

In short, tradition favors kun-SOR-shee-um, analogy with similar words in which TI is pronounced like SH (e.g. *nasturtium, byzantium, nation, partial, patient, tertiary*) justifies it, and general practice still prefers it. See **controversial**, **negotiate**.

consummate (adjective) kun-SUHM-it, not KAHN-suh-mit.

The adjective is pronounced kun-SUHM-it, the verb is pronounced KAHN-suh-mayt.

contemplative kun-TEMP-luh-tiv, not KAHN-tem-play-tiv.

controversial kahn-truh-VUR-shuul. Do not say kahn-truh-VUR-see-al.

In the last few years, the broadcast media have suddenly and almost universally adopted the pronunciation kahn-truh-VUR-see-al (or sometimes kahn-truh-VUR-shee-al), and much of the public has copied their poor example.

The *NBC Handbook* (1984) is not the culprit; it gives only kahn-truh-VUR-shuul, as do *Webster's New World* (1984) and *Random House II* (1987). However, further study reveals that kahn-truh-VUR-see-al and kahn-truh-VUR-shee-al are secreted in *Webster* 3 (1961) but do not reappear as variants until 1985, when *Webster's Ninth* and *American Heritage,* Second College, list them after the traditional kahn-truh-VUR-shuul.

Conclusion? Kahn-truh-VUR-see-al and kahn-truh-VUR-shee-al are vogue pronunciations that got started about thirty years ago, played off-off Broadway until they got a lucky break a few years back and broke into broadcasting. Now they are on all the networks, threatening to take over Civilization As We Know It. My advice? You never know when the winds of trend will change. Stick with kahn-truh-VUR-shuul and no one can stick it to you. See **consortium**, **negotiate** (and also the Appendix for more on Vogue Pronunciations).

coupon KOO-pahn.

The pronunciation KYOO-pahn is widespread, and used by many otherwise conscientious speakers—Vincent Price, for example. Neither analogy nor spelling, however, justifies it. We do not say byoo-TEEK for *boutique,* TYOOR-nuh-kit for *tourniquet,* or uh-KYOO-tur for *accouter,* or insert a Y before the OO sound in *nouveau riche, coup d'état,* and *haute couture.* Why say KYOO-pahn?

Most dictionaries of the last thirty years list KYOO-pahn, but it is not preferred. *Webster* 2 (1934) calls it incorrect.

covert (adjective and noun) KUH-vurt.

The pronunciation KOH-vurt didn't see the light of dictionary until *Webster* 3 included it in 1961. From what I can gather it wasn't around very long before that. My conjecture is that it probably got started during the McCarthy era, when certain folks were worried about spies in the pumpkin patch and under the streets and needed an appropriately ugly and alarming way to pronounce that.

For a decade KOH-vurt lay low, hiding out in the back rooms of Congress and the Pentagon. Then came the Wa-

---

a = at • a̲ = woman • ah = spa • ahr = car • air = fair • ay = hay • aw = saw • ch = chip • e = let • e̲ = item • ee = see • eer = deer • i = sit • i̲ = direct • ng = sing • o̲ = connect • oh = go • oo = soon • or = for • oor = poor • ow = cow • oy = toy • sh = she • th = thin • th̲ = them • u̲ = focus • uh = up • ur = turn • uu = pull, took • y, eye = by, pie • zh = measure

tergate scandal, and people had something really ugly to be alarmed about—it was the good guys in government who were doing all the underhanded stuff! With Watergate, KOH-vurt came out of the closet, paraded itself on radio and television, and made it clear that from now on it would be calling the shots. Since then I don't believe I have heard one broadcaster say KUH-vurt. (Make that one—*me*.) That is indeed alarming.

I know that by recommending KUH-vurt over KOH-vurt (and koh-VURT, which is also popular but listed even less often), I have joined the losing side in the war. Although the ranks have thinned considerably in the last ten years, many faithful troops are still on my side and I will fight this one to the bitter end. Besides, I have always favored the underdog. It's the American way.

P.S.: Here is an update on the conflict. Followers of KOH-vurt include the *NBC Handbook*; *Random House II*; *Webster's Ninth*; *Oxford American*; and *Webster's New World Guide,* which says, with almost elegiac academic courtesy, "The earlier standard pronunciation [KUH-vurt] is heard less frequently now." Current defenders of KUH-vurt include *Webster's New World*; *American Heritage*, New College and Second College editions; *Webster's New Twentieth Century*; *Funk & Wagnalls Standard*; *Scribner–Bantam*; and the *Everyday Reader's Dictionary.*

culinary KYOO-li-ner-ee, not KUHL-i-ner-ee.

The first syllable of this word should sound just like the letter Q: KYOO-li-ner-ee.

Though it has been heard for most of this century, and is quite common today, the pronunciation KUHL-i-ner-ee did not appear in dictionaries until the 1960s. Since then, only Merriam-Webster's wordbooks have put it first; all other sources prefer KYOO-li-ner-ee.

cupola KYOO-po-la.

KYOO-po-la is the only standard pronunciation of this word, which has proved to be quite a tongue twister for many speakers. There are two common mispronunciations to avoid: KYOO-pa-loh, which makes the word sound as if it were spelled *cupalo* (with the A and O transposed), and KOO-pyoo-la, which makes it sound as if it were spelled *coopula*. These ways of saying *cupola* (KYOO-po-la) are not recognized by most dictionaries, and the few that do list them mark them as nonstandard or "unacceptable to many." See **diminution**, **irrelevant**, **jewelry**, **jubilant**, **nuclear**.

D

daiquiri DY-kuh-ree.

This species of rum cocktail was named after Daiquirí, Cuba (Spanish pronunciation: dy-kee-REE), the town where it is said to have originated. The word entered English about 1920, but did not get into a dictionary until the 1950s. By then the alternative pronunciation DAK-ur-ee had caught on, and so from the start was listed in most dictionaries. However, of the sixteen sources I polled, fourteen prefer DY-kuh-ree, with the first syllable pronounced like the word *die,* as it is in Spanish.

dais DAY-is, not DY-is.

This word should be pronounced in two syllables, the first like the word *day* and the second like the word *kiss* without the K. Those who pronounce it DY-is (with the first syllable like the word *die*) are wrong because they treat the A and I not as separate vowels to be sounded distinctly, but as a diphthong with a single sound, as in the word *aisle.* Then, in the second syllable they pronounce the vowel they have already incorporated in the first. Thus, the word would have to be spelled with two I's—*daiis*—to justify the pronunciation DY-is. The one-syllable pronunciation DAYS (rhymes with *lace*) appears in some American dictionaries, but is chiefly British. See **zoology**.

data DAY-tuh, not DAT-uh.

All my sources prefer DAY-tuh. The alternative pronunciation DAT-uh has been recorded since the 1940s, but has always been listed second to DAY-tuh. Another variant, DAH-tuh, is sometimes listed third; it dates back to the nineteenth century or perhaps earlier, and is less frequently heard today.

The reason *data* is pronounced DAY-tuh is because it was taken into English from Latin and follows the rules for the so-called English pronunciation of Latin. According to this method, says *Webster* 2 (1934), "Vowels, when ending accented syllables, have always their long English sounds, as *pater* [PAY-tur], *homo* [HOH-moh]." The first syllable of *data* (*da-*) is accented and ends in the vowel A; therefore, the A is long, as in the word *day*. See **apparatus**, **erratum**, **gratis**, **status**.

decibel DES-i-bel. Do not say DES-i-buul.

The *bel* in this word comes from Alexander Graham Bell. An *ohm* (named after George Simon Ohm) is never called an *um,* nor is a *watt* (named after James Watt) ever called a *what*. The legacy of a man is at stake here. Remember that the E in the last syllable should be as clear as a *bell*.

decrease (noun) DEE-krees; (verb) de-KREES.

In words of two syllables . . . that do double duty as nouns or adjectives on the one hand and as verbs on the other,

---

a = at • a = woman • ah = spa • ahr = car • air = fair • ay = hay •
aw = saw • ch = chip • e = let • e = item • ee = see • eer = deer
• i = sit • i = direct • ng = sing • o = connect • oh = go • oo =
soon • or = for • oor = poor • ow = cow • oy = toy • sh = she •
th = thin • th = them • u = focus • uh = up • ur = turn • uu =
pull, took • y, eye = by, pie • zh = measure

it is the custom, with a few exceptions, to accent the nouns and adjectives upon the *first* syllable and the verbs upon the *last*.

—W. H. P. Phyfe, *18,000 Words Often Mispronounced.*

Phyfe's rule, outlined in 1926, holds true today for many words. Below is a partial list (in which the boldfaced examples appear as separate entries in this book):

Bisyllabic words that function as both nouns, with the accent on the *first* syllable, and verbs, with the accent on the *second* syllable, include abstract, **accent**, addict, affect, affix, ally (some speakers say uh-LY for both noun and verb), annex, combat, compact, compound, compress, console, convert, convict, desert, digest, essay, export, import, incense, **increase**, insert, insult, object, perfume, **permit**, pervert, prefix, presage, present, produce, progress, project, protest, rebel, record, refuse, reject, subject, survey, suspect, torment, **transfer**, and transport.

Bisyllabic words that function as both adjectives, with the accent on the *first* syllable, and verbs, with the accent on the *second* syllable, include absent, **frequent**, perfect, present, and suspect.

Exceptions to the rule—and of course, as with all rules, there are plenty—include access (the verb, which comes from the jargon of computer science and dates back to 1966, is pronounced AK-ses, like the noun), address (for the noun, uh-DRES or A-dres), bias, comment, consent, defeat, defect (for the noun, DEE-fekt or de-FEKT), delay, **deluge**, detail (several dictionaries prefer the accent on the second syllable for both noun and verb), dispute, effect, finance (many speakers use FY-nans or fi-NANS for both noun and verb), format (the verb, a 1964 creation also from computer science, is pronounced FOR-mat, like the noun), **grimace** (traditionally, gri-MAYS for both noun and verb), preface, profile, **program**, recess (properly, re-SES for both noun and verb), report, research (correctly, re-SURCH for both noun and verb), salute, and tutor.

Newscasters are some of the worst offenders of Phyfe's rule, especially with the words *decrease* and *increase,* for which they will shift the accent as it suits them, perhaps prompted by the mistaken notion that to emphasize the contrasting prefixes *in-* and *de-* will ensure comprehension. This is unnecessary, even condescending. Anyone is capable of understanding these and analogous words when they are pronounced properly.

deity DEE-i-tee, not DAY-i-tee. See **homogeneity, spontaneity**.

deluge (noun and verb) DEL-yooj.

This word takes a little practice to pronounce correctly. Difficulty with it has resulted in a DEL-yooj of variants, including DEL-yoozh, DEL-oozh, DEL-ooj, de-LOOJ, and de-LOOZH. Most dictionaries do not list any pronunciation other than DEL-yooj, in which the first syllable is stressed and the second syllable sounds like the word *huge* without the H.

depot DEE-poh.

Many authorities mark the alternative DEP-oh (DEP- rhyming with *step*) as chiefly military and British. American usage has always favored DEE-poh (DEE- rhyming with *see*), and it seems reasonable to use it for all the word's senses.

despicable DES-pik-uh-buul. Now usually duh-SPIK-uh-buul.

DES-pik-uh-buul has been the preferred pronunciation for a hundred years, and duh-SPIK-uh-buul was often labeled incorrect or erroneous until the 1960s, when it became unfashionable for dictionaries to use that sort of word. Despite the popularity of duh-SPIK-uh-buul (perhaps owing in part to the slobbering cartoon character

Daffy Duck's penchant for spitting out the second syllable), most recent sources still pass silent judgment on it and continue to prefer DES-pik-uh-buul, or list only this pronunciation. These include *Funk & Wagnalls Standard* (1980); *Webster's New World* (1984); the *NBC Handbook* (1984); the *American Heritage,* Second College (1985); and *Random House II* (1987). See **explicable**, **hospitable**, **inexplicable**, **lamentable**, **summarily**.

dew DYOO.

There is a tendency in American speech to change the YOO or long U sound in many words to an OO sound (as in *soon*). We are in the process of dropping YOO/long U from such words as *duty, assume, presume, attitude, aptitude, astute, nutrition, student,* and the like. Directly following an initial S, the long U is rarely heard from Americans: We say SOOT for *suit* and SOOPER for *super*; the British say SYOOT and SYOOPER. And directly following an L—in such words as *illusion, illuminate, alluring, flute,* and *absolutely*—the YOO/long U has almost entirely disappeared from cultivated speech on both sides of the Atlantic.

The YOO/long U sound occurs in about half of the handful of English words ending in or incorporating -*ew*. It is intact (for now, anyway) in *few, spew, view, mew, nephew,* and *askew*; it is giving way to OO in *new, knew, stew, mildew,* and *gewgaw*. It would be nice if we took pains to preserve it in these words (with the single exception of *lewd,* which, because -*ew* follows an L, makes YOO/long U sound appropriate only in the mouths of Elizabethan actors).

Most current authorities prefer DOO, but for those speakers whose concern for propriety in speech extends to beauty and harmony, I recommend retaining the cultivated and euphonious DYOO. See **duty**, **new**.

diesel DEE-zuul, not DEE-suul.

DEE-suul has been listed in most dictionaries since the 1960s, but is not preferred.

Diesel comes from Rudolph Diesel, a German automotive engineer. *Webster* 2 (1934), notes that in German the letter S is pronounced "like English S in *rose* at the beginning of a word ... and before a vowel." We should follow this rule when we say *diesel* (DEE-zuul), for it breaks no rule of English nor does it pose any difficulty to the tongue.

diminution di-mi-NYOO-sh<u>i</u>n or di-mi-NOO-sh<u>i</u>n.

This word is often mispronounced dim-yoo-NISH-<u>in</u>, as if it were spelled *dimunition*. See **cupola**, **irrelevant**, **jewelry**, **jubilant**, **nuclear**.

diphtheria dif-THEER-ee-uh, not dip-THEER-ee-uh.

Properly, the PH is pronounced like an F, as in *telephone, phonetics,* and *ophiolatry* (AHF-ee-**AHL**-uh-tree), the worship of snakes. See **diphthong**, **ophthalmologist**.

diphthong DIF-thawng or DIF-thahng, not DIP-thawng.

Both Hs in this word are part of consonant blends with specific, distinct sounds (like BL in *blue,* SH in *ship,* or CH in *chop*). To drop the second H and say DIF-tawng or drop both Hs and say DIP-tawng would not only be wrong,

---

a = at • <u>a</u> = woman • ah = spa • ahr = car • air = fair • ay = hay • aw = saw • ch = chip • e = let • <u>e</u> = item • ee = see • eer = deer • i = sit • <u>i</u> = direct • ng = sing • <u>o</u> = connect • oh = go • oo = soon • or = for • oor = poor • ow = cow • oy = toy • sh = she • th = thin • <u>th</u> = them • <u>u</u> = focus • uh = up • ur = turn • uu = pull, took • y, eye = by, pie • zh = measure

it would sound ridiculous. Yet many otherwise careful speakers seem to think that it is proper to drop the first H and say DIP-thawng. Dictionaries acknowledge their preference, but do not share it. See **diphtheria**, **ophthalmologist**.

dirigible DIR-i-ji-buul.

The alternative pronunciation di-RIJ-i-buul has been listed in American dictionaries since the 1960s, but is not preferred. Kenyon and Knott, in their *Pronouncing Dictionary of American English,* call it British.

disparate DIS-pa-rit, not dis-PAR-it.

If you happen to own *Webster's Ninth,* which prefers dis-PAR-it, with the accent on the second syllable, do not be misled about the proper pronunciation of this word. All my other sources prefer or give only DIS-pa-rit, with the accent on the first syllable.

dissect di-SEKT.

The alternative pronunciations dy-SEKT and DY-sekt (with the first syllable pronounced like the word *die*) were not recognized by dictionaries before the 1960s. In 1961, *Webster* 3 labeled them "unacceptable to many." Most current dictionaries list but do not prefer them, and *Webster's New World Guide* (1984) and the *NBC Handbook* (1984) give only di-SEKT.

It is the double S in *dissect* that makes the I short (like the I in *hit*) rather than long (like the I in *dine*). The word combines the Latin prefix *dis-* with -*sect*, a suffix from the Latin *sectus,* the past participle of *secare,* to cut. It means literally to cut apart, cut up completely. The prefix *dis-* appears in similar words with double S: dissent, dissemble, disserve, dissociate, dissatisfy, disseminate, and dissertation. In all of these, *dis-* rhymes with *kiss*, as it should in *dissect*.

dour DOOR.

Properly, *dour* should rhyme with *poor,* not with *hour*. This is the marking of the *NBC Handbook* (1984); *Webster 2* (1934); the *OED* (1928); *Funk & Wagnalls New Standard* (1980); the *Century* (1914) and *New Century* (1927); and W. H. P. Phyfe (1926). *Dour* is the same as the archaic word *dure,* hard, severe, which goes back through Middle English to the Latin *durus* (DOO-ruus), hard. The pronunciation DOOR (rhyming with *poor*) and the altered spelling of the word come from Scottish.

Many current sources prefer the pronunciation DUUR (UU as in *book,* so that the word almost rhymes with *sir*) or sometimes DOWR (which rhymes with *hour*), and some sources no longer list DOOR (rhymes with *poor*). DUUR may originally have been a regional preference, like RUUM for *room* or RUUF for *roof,* in which the proper OO sound in these words is cut to the UU sound of ROOK. DOWR is fairly recent spelling pronunciation (see Appendix). I favor the traditional pronunciation, of course, and believe that if someone already says DUUR, they can, with little effort, easily lengthen the diphthong to DOOR. Those who say DOWR will have to relearn the word.

drowned DROWND.

This word has one syllable. The pronunciation DROWN-d̲e̲d is nonstandard.

ducat DUHK-it (like *duck* + *it*).

A *ducat* is a type of coin, usually made of gold, formerly used by various European countries. *Ducats* figure prominently in tales and movies about marauders on the bounding main. Don't be misled by Errol Flynn or any other Hollywood swashbucklers who mispronounce this word DOOK-it or DYOOK-it. DUHK-it is the only recognized pronunciation.

duty DYOO-tee.

DYOO-tee, the traditional pronunciation, is preferable to DOO-tee, which is commonly heard today. See **dew**.

E

ebullient i-BUHL-yent or i-BUUL-yent. Not i-BOOL-yent or i-BYOO-lee-ent.

Ebullient should be pronounced in three syllables. In the second, accented syllable (-BUL-), the U may have the sound of the U in *bulk* or *bull*.

either EE-thur.

Though both EE-thur and NEE-thur (EE and NEE rhyming with *see*) and EYE-thur and NY-thur (EYE and NY rhyming with *high*) occur in American and British speech, all sources agree that EE-thur and NEE-thur are the prevailing and customary American pronunciations, and EYE-thur and NY-thur are preferred in contemporary standard British speech.

Webster 2 (1934) notes that EYE-thur "is more prevalent in England (especially in southern England) than in America. In the seventeenth century, the word was pronounced [AY-thur]. . . . Both [EE-thur] and [EYE-thur] were in general use by 1790."

---

a = at • a = woman • ah = spa • ahr = car • air = fair • ay = hay • aw = saw • ch = chip • e = let • e = item • ee = see • eer = deer • i = sit • i = direct • ng = sing • o = connect • oh = go • oo = soon • or = for • oor = poor • ow = cow • oy = toy • sh = she • th = thin • th = them • u = focus • uh = up • ur = turn • uu = pull, took • y, eye = by, pie • zh = measure

In the nineteenth century EYE-<u>th</u>ur and NY-<u>th</u>ur "came to predominate in standard British speech," explains *Random House II* (1987). "In American English, therefore, [they] reflect a recent borrowing from British speech rather than a survival from the time of early settlement, influenced as well by the *ei* spelling, which is pronounced (ī) in such words as *height* and *stein*." EYE-<u>th</u>ur and NY-<u>th</u>ur now "occur occasionally," claims *Random House II*, "chiefly in the speech of the educated and in the network standard English of radio and television."

That EYE-<u>th</u>ur and NY-<u>th</u>ur are recent borrowings from British speech occurring mainly among the educated and in the media raises an interesting question, which *Random House II* leaves unanswered. Why is it that *educated* Americans have adopted British pronunciations for these words? Could it be to draw attention to their education? Speech, like dress, is often a form of social statement. Among certain educated Americans, EYE-<u>th</u>ur and NY-<u>th</u>ur are but two examples of a predilection for British pronunciations, which these speakers apparently imagine will make their opinions seem more respectable or give them the edge on their peers. Students of common sense, however, know that good pronunciation in an American speaker is not necessarily a sign of intelligence, and poor pronunciation in an American speaker is not necessarily a sign of ignorance, but British pronunciation in an American speaker is almost always a sign that someone is putting on the dog. See **neither** and, for more on American versus British pronunciation, **juror**, **paradigm**, **precedence**, **textile**, **vagaries**.

electoral <u>e</u>-LEK-tuh-r<u>a</u>l, not EE-lek-**TOR**-<u>a</u>l.

The accent is on the *second* syllable (-LEK-). See **mayoral**, **pastoral**, **pectoral**.

eleemosynary EL-i-**MAHS**-i-ner-ee.

Standard word division treats the EE in *eleemosynary* as one syllable, not two, and the pronunciation follows by assigning it only one sound. The alternative pronunciation EL-ee-uh-**MAHS**-i-ner-ee, which adds a syllable to the word, is listed in most dictionaries, but is not preferred.

elephantine EL-uh-**FAN**-teen or EL-uh-**FAN**-tin or EL-uh-**FAN**-tyn.

EL-uh-**FAN**-teen is preferred by most current dictionaries, including *Webster's Ninth, Webster's New World,* and *Random House II*. EL-uh-**FAN**-tin is my favorite; it is the preference of older American dictionaries, and is still listed first in several of my recent sources. EL-uh-**FAN**-tyn is originally British (a long I, as in *wine,* for the suffix *-ine* is the usual British pronunciation); it is listed second or third in most current dictionaries.

Avoid the pronunciations EL-uh-fan-tyn and EL-uh-fan-teen, with the accent on the first rather than the third syllable. They are recent variants, listed in a few current dictionaries, but always after one or more of the three pronunciations recommended above.

enclave EN-klayv, not AHN-klayv. See **envelope**, **envoy**.

envelope (noun) EN-vuh-lohp, not AHN-vuh-lohp.

Kenyon and Knott (1949), note that AHN-vuh-lohp (AHN-as in *on*) is "pseudo-French." This is probably why, in the fifty or sixty years it has been listed in dictionaries, AHN-vuh-lohp has never beaten out EN-vuh-lohp for preferred pronunciation status. All my sources give EN-vuh-lohp first. See **enclave**, **envoy.**

envoy EN-voy, not AHN-voy.

AHN-voy (AHN- as in *on*) is "pseudo-French." It is not preferred, and sometimes not even listed. See **envelope.**

equanimity EE-kwuh-**NIM**-i-tee, not EK-wuh-**NIM**-i-tee.

Only two of my sources, *Webster's New World* (1984) and *Webster's New World Guide* (1984), prefer EK-wuh-**NIM**-i-tee. The initial E should be long, as in *equal,* not short, as in *exit.*

equilibrate Traditionally, EE-kwi-**LY**-brayt. Now usually i-KWIL-uh-brayt.

Equilibrate means to balance, bring into equilibrium. The pronunciation i-KWIL-uh-brayt has existed for perhaps seventy or eighty years, but did not appear in dictionaries until 1934. From then until 1961, authorities continued to prefer EE-kwi-**LY**-brayt, but after that date (which is when *Webster* 3 gave i-KWIL-uh-brayt precedence), only one of my sources prefers EE-kwi-**LY**-brayt, and two current dictionaries do not list it at all.

era EER-uh. Do not say E-ruh or AIR-uh.

The first syllable is pronounced like the word *ear.* E-ruh is now often listed, but not preferred. AIR-uh, as far as I know, does not appear in any dictionary.

err UR. Do not say AIR.

This word should rhyme with *her* and *sir,* not with *hair* and *fair.*

"Though [AIR] is now common," says *Webster's New World Guide* (1984), which prudently prefers UR, "it is still objected to by some." What an understatement! In my book, AIR for *err* is right up there in the competition for the Great Beastly Mispronunciation of All Time. While those who don't know how it should be pronounced are blissfully AIRING and being YOOMAN, the beleaguered legions of those who will not forgive fight a divine battle to preserve what has abided for generations. (All right, it's not really a Holy War, just a beastly mispronunciation. Here's the situation.)

Some argue that *err* is etymologically connected to the words *error* and *errant,* and so should be pronounced similarly. This does not cut the mustard, because to draw such a parallel now, after UR has been the only recognized pronunciation since time immemorial, is pedantic and sophistical, a feeble attempt to find a legitimate reason for a mistake—a kind of "he made me do it" excuse. Besides, those who say AIR have not *decided* to say the word this way; they are not etymologists or orthoepists or grammarians who have come to the conclusion that AIR is now correct, nor are they bumpkins who have mystically arrived at a defensible resolution to a long-standing idiosyncrasy of English pronunciation. They are average educated citizens who, in mispronouncing *err,* are simply copying others who they have heard mispronounce it, without so much as a peek into a dictionary to see if what they have embraced is right.

AIR did not appear in a dictionary until the 1960s, and despite its rapid rise to popularity, most current authorities still prefer UR. These include the *American Heritage,* Second College (1985); *Everyday Reader's* (1985); *Webster's New World* (1984); and *Random House II* (1987). Only three of my sources prefer AIR: the *NBC Handbook* (1984), *Webster's Ninth* (1985), and *Webster 3* (1961).

As you may have surmised, we are at a critical point in

---

a = at • a̲ = woman • ah = spa • ahr = car • air = fair • ay = hay • aw = saw • ch = chip • e = let • e̲ = item • ee = see • eer = deer • i = sit • i̲ = direct • ng = sing • o̲ = connect • oh = go • oo = soon • or = for • oor = poor • ow = cow • oy = toy • sh = she • th = thin • th̲ = them • u̲ = focus • uh = up • ur = turn • uu = pull, took • y, eye = by, pie • zh = measure

our controversy over this word. If we do not conscientiously continue to *err* (UR) today, our children surely will *err* (AIR) tomorrow, for as William Safire has said, "In pronunciation and ultimately in usage, when enough of us are wrong, we're right." I'm not sure I agree with that, but I'll admit it's hard to argue.

erratum i-RAY-tum. **errata** (plural) i-RAY-tuh.

Do not say i-RAT-um. The pronunciation e-RAH-tuum, which is sometimes heard, is classical Latin, not English.

The proper pronunciation of *erratum* and *errata* follows the rule for the English pronunciation of Latin explained under **data.** See also **apparatus, status.**

erudite Traditionally, E-roo-dyt. Now usually AIR-yoo-dyt.

Dictionaries began giving AIR-yoo-dyt as an alternative pronunciation in the 1930s and 1940s, and most current dictionaries prefer it. The reason I choose to fight the lonely fight for E-roo-dyt, standing on the burning deck as all make for the lifeboats (to borrow a phrase from Mr. Safire again), is because of my nagging suspicion that it has always been those members of society who would fashion themselves as fashionable who thought it better to say AIR-yoo-dite, though you will never hear them taking pains to pronounce the long U in *duty* or *assume,* or saying the DYOO (*dew*) has fallen rather than the DOO has fallen.

AIR-yoo-dyt was once a vogue pronunciation (see Appendix). That it is now accepted does not obliterate the fact that those who introduced it fifty or sixty years ago and those who readily adopted it were just as desperate and misguided in their search for cultivation as those who today rush to embrace the vogue kahn-truh-VUR-see-al and ne-GOH-see-ayt for the traditional kahn-truh-VUR-shuul and ne-GOH-shee-ayt. See **controversial, negotiate**.

et cetera ET SET-uh-ruh. EK SE-truh is a beastly mispronunciation.

Careful speakers clearly pronounce the T in *et,* and make sure that *cetera* has three syllables.

evil EE-vuul. Do not say EE-vil.

The second syllable (-vil) rhymes with *full,* not *hill.*

In *18,000 Words Often Mispronounced* (1926), W. H. P. Phyfe writes: "Some persons, desiring to seem exact in pronunciation, pronounce this word ē-vĭl. It displays as much ignorance to introduce a sound that is superfluous as to neglect one that is requisite."

evolution EV-uh-**LOO**-shin.

The pronunciation EE-vuh-**LOO**-shin is British.

explicable EK-spli-kuh-buul. Now often ek-SPLIK-uh-buul.

EK-spli-kuh-buul, with the accent on the first syllable, was the only pronunciation listed in dictionaries until the 1960s, when *Webster* 3 gave precedence to ek-SPLIK-uh-buul, which moves the accent to the second syllable. EK-spli-kuh-buul is still preferred by most current authorities, however, including *Random House II,* the *NBC Handbook,* and *Webster's New World.* It is the only pronunciation given in both college editions of the *American Heritage.*

I have always suspected that some pronunciations are preferred simply because they are challenging, and because there is a certain satisfaction in mastering them. EK-spli-kuh-buul is one of these. It takes a cultivated speaker to say it right, and by that I do not mean a highbrow or pretentious speaker, but a trained, practiced, careful one. (Please see the Appendix for more on the subject of Cultivated Speech.)

If you are unaccustomed to saying EK-spli-kuh-buul,

give it a try right now. Hit the first syllable, EK-, extra hard, and let the rest roll off your tongue. You may have some trouble at first, but don't give up. With a little practice it will become easy and natural, and you will leave the expectorating sayers of ek-SPLIK-uh-buul in the dust. See **despicable**, **hospitable**, **inexplicable**, **lamentable**, **summarily**.

exquisite EKS-kwi-zit, not ek-SKWIZ-it.

The accent is properly on the *first* syllable.

Like many mispronunciations, ek-SKWIZ-it got started as a vogue pronunciation (see Appendix), adopted first by those who thought they knew better (or who wanted others to think so) and then picked up by those who didn't know any better than to imitate this *soi-disant* smart set. The quaint charm of accenting the second syllable for added emphasis has long since worn off, however, and the final proof of the banality of the practice is that it failed to wreak havoc in the dictionaries. EKS-kwi-zit is still the preference of nearly all current authorities.

extraordinary ek-STROR-di-ner-ee, not EKS-truh-**OR**-di-ner-ee.

Yes, the word is spelled *extra-ordinary,* and the spelling pronunciation EKS-truh-**OR**-di-ner-ee has been listed in dictionaries for a long time, but you shouldn't say it that way. Why not? Because custom, good usage, authority, and all those important standard-setters have long since settled on ek-STROR-di-ner-ee as the preferred pronunciation.

There is one exception: When *extraordinary* is used in the sense of "beyond the ordinary official duties of"or "sent upon an unusual or special mission," as, an ambassador or minister *extraordinary,* some dictionaries say it is permissible to pronounce the word in six syllables. This meaning is not used very often, though, which is another reason why the five-syllable ek-STROR-di-ner-ee prevails. I recommend it for all senses of the word.

F

February FEB-roo-er-ee. Do not say FEB-yoo-er-ee.

Recently, certain dictionaries have gone to great lengths in their pronunciation notes on this word to tell you that a fancy linguistic process called dissimilation is at work here, in which similar sounds that follow closely in a word tend to become dissimilar, the result being that most educated speakers now replace the first R in *February* with a Y and say FEB-yoo-er-ee.

That is a very convenient explanation, which makes a mispronunciation look right because so many people use it, and makes the correct pronunciation look wrong because only a few people are careful to say the word properly. For some reason current dictionaries love to make elaborate excuses for errors of this nature, perhaps because it makes people feel better and sells more dictionaries.

This book, however, was written on the assumption that you are an educated speaker who has consulted these pages not for encouragement to adopt the next person's whims, copy your neighbor's mistakes, or follow one authority blindly, but to obtain information on the opinions of various authorities and find advice on what pronunciation is best and why, especially in situations where more than one pronunciation exists or there is a controversy over how or how not to say a word.

Therefore, I will not dissemble about dissimilation, or feed you some malarkey about how FEB-yoo-er-ee is an alternative pronunciation based on analogy with January. The fact is that February is a different month, with a peculiar spelling, a peculiar pronunciation, and a very peculiar number of days, all of which adds up to the fact that we must treat the creature with particular respect.

The correct pronunciation, FEB-roo-er-ee, is hard to say, and so most people say FEB-yoo-er-ee because it is easier, not because it is right. As far as the dictionaries are concerned, this is enough to make it a standard pronunciation. As far as this book is concerned, however, FEB-yoo-er-ee may now be standard, but it is still beastly. Regardless of the dissimulations of some, nearly all my sources prefer FEB-roo-er-ee, and as long as careful speakers exist, this is the pronunciation they will prefer. (With a month like February, you can make that kind of leap of faith.) See **library**.

fetid FET-id.

The first syllable (fet-) rhymes with *pet*.

FET-id is the preferred American pronunciation. Most dictionaries also give FEE-tid (FEE- as in *see*), which some mark as chiefly British. FEE-tid probably comes from the alternative spelling *foetid,* which is now rare in American orthography.

finis FIN-is. Occasionally, FY-nis. Fee-NEE is wrong.

Finis means the end. It comes through Middle English from the Latin *finis* (Latin pronunciation FEE-nis or FY-nis). *Finis* is often mistakenly thought to be French, which is why so many mispronounce it fee-NEE.

flaccid FLAK-sid, not FLAS-id.

In 1961, *Webster* 3 recognized FLAS-id, marking it as un-acceptable to many. However, the symbol ÷, used by Merriam-Webster to apprise the reader of a controversial pronunciation, was apparently lost on most people, for today FLAS-id is very common (though among careful speakers no less unacceptable). Five of my current sources list it, and one of these, *Webster's Ninth,* prefers it. This capitulation is unfortunate but inevitable, for when so many insist on mispronouncing a word, dictionaries must eventually recognize the mispronunciation as standard. Most, however, do so reluctantly, as in this case, where it took twenty years for FLAS-id to gain some measure of acceptance.

Flaccid is a book-learned word, which many educated speakers of the last twenty years apparently did not realize (or bother to find out) is traditionally, and by analogy, pronounced FLAK-sid. No literate speaker free of speech impediments says *assident* for *accident, susseed* for *succeed, assept* for *accept,* or *essentric* for *eccentric,* and what goes for these common words holds true for *flaccid.* In these and similar words (where *cc* precedes a vowel), the double C should be pronounced like an X or like KS, as in *accentuate*; *accede*; *occidental*; *succedaneum* (SUHK-suh-**DAY**-nee-u̱m), a substitute; and so on. See **accessory**, **succint**.

flutist FLOO-tist.

The word *flutist* was created in 1603, and FLOO-tist has been and is still the only pronunciation for it. The variant *flautist* was adopted from Italian in 1860, probably because of the influence of Mozart's *Il Flauto Magico* and nineteenth-century Italian opera. The preferred pronunciation for *flautist* is FLAW-tist (FLAW- rhyming with *jaw*); the variant FLOW-tist (FLOW- rhyming with *cow*) is recognized by several of my recent sources but only the *NBC Handbook* prefers it. Unless you have some special or personal reason for preferring Italian spellings and pronunciations, stick with the English *flutist* (FLOO-tist), which is traditional and utterly unaffected.

forbade for-BAD or fur-BAD. Do not say for-BAYD.

Forbade is the past tense of the verb to *forbid*. It is sometimes spelled *forbad,* perhaps in an attempt to make the spelling conform with the proper pronunciation. The spelling pronunciation for-BAYD is now often recognized but is not preferred. The word should be spelled *forbade* and pronounced for-BAD. See **bade**, **brooch**, **joust**.

formidable FOR-mid-uh-buul, not for-MID-uh-buul.

The accent is on the *first* syllable. The beastly mispronunciation for-MID-uh-buul, which shifts the accent to the second syllable, is a FOR-mid-uh-buul one. It has been criticized in pronunciation guides for decades, but doesn't seem to go away. On the other hand, it hasn't gained much attention in the dictionaries either. Say FOR-mid-uh-buul.

forte (strong point) FORT.

When *forte* means a strong point, something at which a person excels, it should be pronounced in one syllable, FORT. (The word comes from the French *fort,* strong, which is also pronounced in one syllable, though without the T sound at the end.) FORT is the traditional pronunciation for this meaning of the word, and is still preferred by all my current sources. See **forte** (music).

forte (music) FOR-tay. Do not say for-TAY.

The musical term *forte,* which comes from Italian, is pronounced FOR-tay, like the Italian. The accent should be on the first syllable. The pronunciation for-TAY (for either the musical term or for the meaning "strong point") is wrong. See **forte** (strong point).

foyer FOY-ur.

This word came into English from French in 1859. The original French pronunciation, still listed in some dictionaries but rarely heard, is fwah-YAY. The half-anglicized pronunciation, FOY-ay (or sometimes foy-YAY), still has many adherents, some of whom maintain that the fully anglicized pronunciation, FOY-ur, is wrong. FOY-ur has existed for most of this century, however, and has been the prevailing pronunciation for at least forty years (Kenyon and Knott gave it precedence in the 1940s).

Anglicization—the process by which words taken from other languages gradually conform to English standards of spelling, usage, and pronunciation—is natural and necessary. Moreover, it is inevitable if the word is to remain in the language. Fwah-YAY, the French pronunciation of *foyer,* is no longer intelligible to most English speakers. FOY-ay, the half-anglicized or hybrid pronunciation, is understandable, and certainly not wrong; it has simply been superseded, as it should be, by the fully anglicized FOY-ur. See **cadre**, **junta**, **lingerie**.

---

a = at • a̲ = woman • ah = spa • ahr = car • air = fair • ay = hay • aw = saw • ch = chip • e = let • e̲ = item • ee = see • eer = deer • i = sit • i̲ = direct • ng = sing • o̲ = connect • oh = go • oo = soon • or = for • oor = poor • ow = cow • oy = toy • sh = she • th = thin • th̲ = them • u̲ = focus • uh = up • ur = turn • uu = pull, took • y, eye = by, pie • zh = measure

frequent (adjective) FREE-kw<u>e</u>nt; (verb) free-KWENT.

Properly, the adjective is accented on the first syllable and the verb on the second. FREE-kw<u>e</u>nt for the verb is common, but incorrect. See **decrease**.

fungi (plural of *fungus*) FUHN-jy. Do not say FUHN-jee, FUHNG-gy, or FUHNG-gee.

Fungus has a hard G, as in *guess*: FUHNG-g<u>u</u>s. *Fungi,* the plural of *fungus,* has a soft G, as in *age,* and a long I, as in *high*: FUHN-jy.

gala GAY-luh.

GAY-luh is preferred by all my current sources. GAL-uh is usually listed next, and GAH-luh, which often appears third, is British, says *Random House II.*

gaseous GAS-ee-us.

GAS-ee-us (pronounced like *gassy* + *us*) is the preferred pronunciation. GASH-us is the most popular alternative in current dictionaries.

Gawain (Sir) GAH-win.

There are almost as many ways to say the name of this legendary knight and nephew to King Arthur as there were seats at the Round Table. In *How I Grew,* the first volume of her autobiography, Mary McCarthy insists that the proper pronunciation is GOW-wayn (GOW- accented and rhyming with *cow,* and -wayn as in the name *Wayne*). I would be interested to know on what authority she based her preference, for GOW-wayn is the one variant that does not appear in any of my sources. GOW-win, which comes close, is listed third in two current dictionaries.

The pronunciation most often preferred by past and present authorities is GAH-win. Out of sixteen sources polled, seven put it first, four second. GAH-wayn is the runner-up, with four dictionaries putting it first and two second. Third place goes to GAW-win (GAW- rhyming with *saw*), with four second-place listings and one first. The variant guh-WAYN, which is now very often heard, is the only pronunciation that places the accent on the second syllable. Its popularity has led two current dictionaries to prefer it, but it is not listed in any sources printed before 1982.

genuine JEN-yoo-in.

Do not say JEN-yoo-wyn (-wyn as in *wine*). This pronunciation has always been stigmatized. Those who use it are looked upon by many as careless or uneducated speakers, or as caricaturing them. In *Everyday Errors in Pronunciation,* published in 1936, John G. Gilmartin advises us to "remember that, though *wine* is now legal, *gen u wine* is not and never has been."

gibberish JIB-ur-ish.

The alternative pronunciation GIB-ur-ish, with a hard G as in *go,* was at one time preferred. It is still the usual British pronunciation. Since the 1930s, JIB-ur-ish, with a soft G as in *gesture,* has been favored by American dictionaries, and GIB-ur-ish is now rarely heard in the United States.

giblet JIB-lit, not GIB-lit.

glaucoma glaw-COH-muh (glaw- as in *law*).

The variant pronunciation glow-COH-muh (glow- rhyming with *cow*) did not appear in dictionaries until the 1960s; it is now listed first in several recent sources. I do not recommend it because it is based on an incorrect judgment of how to pronounce the vowel combination AU.

In English, AU is occasionally pronounced as a **diphthong** (DIF-thawng), which *Webster* 2 defines as "a continuous glide from one sound to another," but in nearly all of the words in which it appears it is pronounced as a digraph (DY-graf), which *Webster* 2 calls "two letters spelling a single vowel, as in beat, group, laud."

AU is a diphthong (with the gliding sound of OW as in *out*) in *umlaut* and *sauerkraut*. AU is a digraph (with the sound of AW as in *saw*) in *sauce, taut, caught, applaud, flaunt, maudlin,* etc., and in practically every word it initiates: *author, audience, automobile, autochthonous,* and so on.

There are a great many more English words in which AU is treated as a digraph, and properly *glaucoma* is among them. Glow-COH-muh (glow- rhyming with *how* and *now*) is popular but eccentric; glaw-COH-muh (glaw- rhyming with *saw* and *law*) is traditional and consistent with analogous words. See **flutist** (which discusses *flautist*), **trauma**.

gondola GAHN-do-la, not gahn-DOH-la.

The stress should be on the *first* syllable.

In the movie *Heartburn,* based on Nora Ephron's book, a woman says, "Arthur's idea of romance is Venice, *gon*dolas," stressing the first syllable. "Gon*do*las," her husband interrupts, stressing the second syllable in an irritated tone of voice that implies he has corrected her often. "Yes, of course," she says, and changes the subject.

This is precisely the sort of unfortunate situation I had in mind when I decided to write this book, and I hope you will use what is written here as ammunition in your

a = at • a = woman • ah = spa • ahr = car • air = fair • ay = hay • aw = saw • ch = chip • e = let • e = item • ee = see • eer = deer • i = sit • i = direct • ng = sing • o = connect • oh = go • oo = soon • or = for • oor = poor • ow = cow • oy = toy • sh = she • th = thin • th = them • u = focus • uh = up • ur = turn • uu = pull, took • y, eye = by, pie • zh = measure

defense should you become the victim of erroneous correction. Correcting someone's pronunciation (or grammar or diction or anything else) can be one of the most obnoxious things a person can do, but it doesn't have to be. When I find myself impelled to do it, I try to follow these two rules:

1. Don't ever interrupt the speaker. Make your comments later, and, if possible, in private.
2. Make damn sure you're right!

In this case the woman was right to put the accent on the *gon-* in *gondola,* and her partner, who apparently had never checked the pronunciation in a dictionary, broke both rules and made an ass of himself.

Gahn-DOH-la, with the accent on the second syllable, has been heard since about 1920, but was not recognized by dictionaries until the 1960s. It is still listed second in current dictionaries. In the last few years, as gahn-DOH-la has become more popular, a debate has arisen over when it is appropriate to use it. *Random House II* (1987) prefers the pronunciation GAHN-do-la, but adds that gahn-DOH-la is used especially for the boat we associate with the canals of Venice. However, *Webster's New World Guide* (1984) asserts that GAHN-do-la "is usual for the boat" and gahn-DOH-la "is more common for other meanings." *Webster's Ninth* (1985) also cites GAHN-do-la as the customary pronunciation for the boat.

The debate seems somewhat ridiculous, for ultimately the point is this: Whether you say gahn-DOH-la for the boat, the car, or any of the other meanings, you've missed the boat. Current sources prefer GAHN-do-la, with the accent on the first syllable, and the older ones give only this pronunciation.

government GUHV-urn-ment.

Try to preserve the N in *government,* pronouncing the second syllable URN rather than UR. (Regional speakers who normally drop their Rs—pronouncing *arm* as AHM or *farther* as FAH-thur, for example—would say GUHV-un-ment.)

The pronunciations GUH-vur-ment, GUH-vuh-ment, and GUHV-ment, in which the N is not articulated, are all standard, and have been so for at least fifty years. In the 1940s, Kenyon and Knott wrote that "no competent observer can doubt [their] prevalence . . . among the leading statesmen of US and England, even in formal public address." This is true; however, most current sources continue to prefer GUHV-urn-ment with the N, and conscientious speakers still pronounce it this way.

gramercy gruh-MUR-see.

Gramercy is an archaic interjection used to express surprise or thanks. It is a contraction of the phrase *grand mercy,* which is why the accent falls on the second syllable, the mer- of *mercy:* gruh-MUR-see. For Gramercy Park in New York City, however, the customary pronunciation is GRAM-ur-see (like *grammar* + *see*), with the stress on the first syllable. See **Carnegie**.

granary Properly, GRAN-a-ree. Popularly, GRAY-na-ree.

Look this word up in a number of dictionaries and you will see something curious: some divide it *gran·a·ry,* the first syllable being gran-; others divide it *gra·na·ry,* with the first syllable gra-. Now, if you look closely you will see that the ones that mark the first syllable gran- prefer the pronunciation GRAN-a-ree (*Webster 2; Funk & Wagnalls Standard; American Heritage,* Second College; and *Webster's New World*), and the ones that mark it gra- prefer the pronunciation GRAY-na-ree (*Webster 3; Webster's Ninth;* and *Random House II*). Of course there are a few dic-

tionaries that divide the word gra·na·ry and prefer GRAN-
-a-ree, or divide it gran·a·ry and prefer GRAY-na-ree, but
that's goofy. Perhaps at the root of the problem is the
word *grainery,* which appears in *Webster* 2 and *Webster*
3 with the pronunciation GRAYN-a-ree. This variant, which
Webster 2 calls Southern, is rarely used, but its pronunciation has steadily become attached to *granary.*

And so the controversy rages in the dictionaries, and
there is no way to resolve it but to take sides. If you think
pronunciation should reflect meaning, and that word division should reflect pronunciation, imagine that *granary*
comes from the English *grain,* divide it gra·na·ry, and say
GRAY-na-ree. If you favor traditional pronunciations and
respect the influence of etymology, remember that the word
comes from the Latin *granarium,* divide it gran·a·ry, and
say GRAN-a-ree. With the former, you won't be wrong,
but with the latter, you'll have a few more sources to back
you up.

gratis GRAT-is or GRAY-tis. Do not say GRAH-tis.

Gratis comes directly from Latin and means free, without
charge. GRAT-is (GRAT- rhyming with *cat*) is preferred
by all my current sources. GRAY-tis (GRAY- as in the color),
which was formerly preferred, is now listed second; it
represents the so-called English pronunciation of Latin.
GRAH-tis (with the Italian A, as in *father* or *harp*) is the
classical Latin pronunciation; in other words, it conforms
to the way scholars have reckoned the ancient Romans
spoke their language and the way Latin is now taught in
schools. GRAH-tis is not listed in dictionaries. See **data**
(for more on the English pronunciation of Latin words).

grievous GREE-vus, not GREE-vee-us.

Be sure to say this word in *two,* not three syllables, like
a combination of the words *grieve* and *us.* See **mischievous**, **heinous**, **intravenous**.

grimace Traditionally, gri-MAYS (-MAYS rhymes with FACE). Now usually GRIM-is.

Here is the story of how a gri-MAYS became a GRIM-is. The noun *grimace* came into the language in the mid-seventeenth century, the verb came along in the mid-eighteenth century, and for nearly two hundred years after that the only pronunciation for both was gri-MAYS. In the late 1940s, *American College* recognized GRIM-is, and in 1961, *Webster* 3 gave it precedence. Then came the inane McDonald's restaurant advertising campaign with Ronald McDonald and his puppet sidekick GRIM-is, and poor old gri-MAYS became as strange as a square hamburger. The only current sources I can find that still prefer gri-MAYS are *Webster's New World* (1984) and *Webster's New World Guide* (1984).

One of the tragic aspects of capriciously changing the pronunciation of an old, established word is the loss of its conventional rhythm and rhyme. Gri-MAYS rhymes easily with many words, and its pleasing iambic meter—with a short syllable followed by a long one—is the most common foot in English poetry. GRIM-is, with its obscure second syllable and heavier trochaic meter—a long syllable followed by a short one—is virtually impossible to rhyme.

The Painful Case of Poor Grimace

Gri*mace* is dead! Long live gri*mace*!
*Grim*ace has usurped its place.
Defiant of three hundred years,

---

a = at • a̲ = woman • ah = spa • ahr = car • air = fair • ay = hay • aw = saw • ch = chip • e = let • e̲ = item • ee = see • eer = deer • i = sit • i̲ = direct • ng = sing • o̲ = connect • oh = go • oo = soon • or = for • oor = poor • ow = cow • oy = toy • sh = she • th = thin • t̲h̲ = them • u̲ = focus • uh = up • ur = turn • uu = pull, took • y, eye = by, pie • zh = measure

An upstart strain has seized our ears,
And twisted English to its limits,
Declaring: "There's no rhyme for *grim*ace!"

This offspring of recessive stress,
Transfixed us with its ugliness;
It warped its rhythm, shed its rhyme,
Became a fixture on prime time.
Though what we saw and what we heard
Was not the real or proper word,
Still all rushed headlong to embrace
This modish *grim*ace—good-bye, gri*mace*!

Gri*mace* is dead! Long live gri*mace*!
*Grim*ace has usurped its place.
The arriviste has put a curse
Upon all English prose and verse,
And left our writers but the dimmest,
Slimmest hope of rhyming *grim*aced.

But such is life in the language game,
Where nothing seems to stay the same.
Tomorrow will today erase:
*Grim*ace is in, gone is gri*mace*.
Yet, friend—in secret, unobserved,
I vow to see tradition served—
When I put on a nasty face,
I'll still call it a gri*mace*.

grovel GRAH-v<u>e</u>l or GRUH-v<u>e</u>l.

Both are standard pronunciations. GRAH-v<u>e</u>l was preferred by older dictionaries, and GRUH-v<u>e</u>l was not recognized until *Webster* 2 included it in 1934. Kenyon and
Knott (1949) note that the pronunciation GRUH-v<u>e</u>l "shows
the original vowel" and GRAH-v<u>e</u>l is a spelling pronunciation. Sources since then are about evenly divided. See
hovel.

guillotine GIL-uh-teen, not GEE-yuh-teen. (Pronounce the Ls.)

This word came into English in 1793 and quickly became anglicized. Noah Webster's dictionary of 1841 gives the pronunciation GIL-uh-tin; Worcester's dictionary of 1884 marks it gil-uh-TEEN, with the accent on the final syllable. By the early twentieth century, authorities had generally settled on GIL-uh-teen, which, for the noun, is the preference of all my current sources, though for the verb some authorities still prefer gil-uh-TEEN.

The variant pronunciation GEE-yuh-teen, with the Ls silent, is a de-anglicization that has existed for only about thirty years. The word has long been anglicized and the Ls should be pronounced. See **cadre** (for a discussion of anglicization and de-anglicization).

H

handkerchief HANG-kur-chif. Do not say HANG-kur-cheef.

HANG-kur-chif is universally preferred. HANG-kur-cheef (-cheef as in *chief*) is a spelling pronunciation (see the Appendix for a discussion of this term).

harass HAR-is or ha-RAS.

HAR-is is pronounced like the name *Harris*. The accent is on the first syllable and the word rhymes with *embarrass*. Ha-RAS, with the accent on the second syllable, rhymes with *alas*.

Both pronunciations are now standard in America. HAR-is is the traditional one, dating back to the seventeenth century when the word came into English from French; ha-RAS has been heard for about a hundred years. In 1909, *Webster's New International* noted that the word was "often pronounced [ha-RAS], but this has never been countenanced by orthoepists." In 1934, *Webster* 2 recognized ha-RAS; in 1949, Kenyon and Knott observed that "[ha-RAS] instead of the older [HAR-is] appears to be on the increase"; and in 1961, *Webster* 3 gave ha-RAS precedence. According to *Random House II* (1987), ha-RAS is now more common in the United States, "especially among younger educated speakers, some of whom have only minimal familiarity with the older form."

As a "younger educated speaker" growing up in New York City in the 1960s, I had always heard ha-RAS (and believe me, living in that city I heard it a great deal). One evening I turned on the news and for the first time heard the word pronounced HAR-is. Apparently someone in the newsroom had gotten hold of a dictionary and discovered that HAR-is was the traditional pronunciation, which I found out moments later when I hastened to the family dictionary (*Webster* 2) to check it myself. For some time after that, broadcasters around the country seemed to favor HAR-is, but now its occurrence on the air has fallen off, and ha-RAS is once again commonly heard.

Some who say HAR-is (now perhaps mostly older speakers) are irritated by those who say ha-RAS. To take umbrage, however, is unfair, because ha-RAS is now acceptable and because it is the proper role of the young to vex the old. With this word, I say do as you will and live and let live. I say HAR-is, mainly to be consistent in my preference for traditional pronunciations, but also to nettle anyone who insists the word must be pronounced ha-RAS.

height HYT (rhymes with *night*).

It is incorrect to pronounce this word with a TH sound at the end. Do not say HYT-TH (like *height* + *th*) or HYTH. These are dialectal pronunciations, which arose during the several centuries when the word's spelling was variable; Milton, for example, spelled it *highth,* and Shakespeare, whose spelling was inconsistent, often used *hight*.

---

a = at • a = woman • ah = spa • ahr = car • air = fair • ay = hay • aw = saw • ch = chip • e = let • e = item • ee = see • eer = deer • i = sit • i = direct • ng = sing • o = connect • oh = go • oo = soon • or = for • oor = poor • ow = cow • oy = toy • sh = she • th = thin • th = them • u = focus • uh = up • ur = turn • uu = pull, took • y, eye = by, pie • zh = measure

"Current usage is a compromise," says the *OED*, "retaining the spelling *height* (which has been by far the most frequent written form since 1500), with the pronunciation of *hight*."

To all who say HYT-TH or HYTH, I make this appeal: Your day is long past; stop being perverse and go with the flow. Besides, what can you rhyme it with when you pronounce it that way?

heinous HAY-n<u>i</u>s.

Do not say HEE-n<u>i</u>s or HEE-nee-<u>i</u>s (HEE- as in *heat*), both of which are HAY-n<u>i</u>s and longstanding members of the Most Unwanted Beastly Mispronunciations List. *Heinous* has two syllables, and the first is pronounced like the word *hay*. See **mischievous**, **grievous**, **intravenous**.

helicopter HEL-<u>i</u>-KAHP-tur, not **HEE**-l<u>i</u>-KAHP-tur.

herb URB. (Do not pronounce the H.)

"The historical pronunciation is [URB]," says *Webster* 2 (1934), "which still prevails in the best usage in the United States, although [HURB] is also used. In England [HURB] has increased in use since about 1800, and now apparently prevails in the best usage."

According to the *Century Dictionary* (1914), "The initial H, as regular in words coming from Latin through Old French, was silent in Middle English and is properly silent in Modern English, but is now sometimes pronounced, in conformity to *herbaceous, herbarium,* and other forms in which the H is properly pronounced, as being recently taken from the Latin."

The initial H should be pronounced in *herbal* (now frequently pronounced URB-<u>a</u>l, without the H), *herbalist, herbicide, herbaceous, herbivore, herbivorous,* and *herbarium*—all Modern English words derived directly from Latin. It is properly silent only in the older, Middle English words *herbage* and *herb*.

homicide HAHM-i̱-syd, not HOHM-i̱-syd.

The hom- in *homicide* should rhyme with *Tom,* not with *comb*.

The Latin root of *homicide* is *homicida*, a murderer, a word used by the poet Horace of the Trojan warrior Hector to mean "slayer of men." *Homicida* comes in turn from *homo,* man, and *caedere,* to cut. In Latin, the O in the hom- of *homicida* and *homo* was short, as in *dog,* and this short vowel, anglicized slightly from roughly an AW to an AH sound, has been retained in the preferred pronunciation: HAHM-i̱-syd.

Dictionaries divide the word *hom·i·cide*, which reflects the proper pronunciation. *Webster's Ninth* idiosyncratically divides it *ho·mi·cide*, but also gives the pronunciation HAHM-i̱-syd first.

homogeneity HOH-moh-ji̱-**NEE**-i̱-tee, not HOH-moh-ji̱-**NAY**-i-tee.

The accented antepenultimate syllable (-ne-) of *homogeneity* should be pronounced NEE (like *knee*), with a long E, not with the long A sound of *nay*. See **deity**, **spontaneity**.

hospitable HAHS-pit-uh-buul, not hah-SPIT-uh-buul.

This word is now so frequently mispronounced that one current dictionary (*Webster's Ninth*) has capitulated and listed hah-SPIT-uh-buul first. My other sources, however, all prefer the accent on the first syllable, as in *hospital,* and *Webster 2* (1934) calls hah-SPIT-uh-buul chiefly British.

One advantage to saying this word properly is that you avoid stressing the *spit* part of the word, which, considering the word's meaning, sounds rather *inHOSpitable*.

See **despicable**, **explicable**, **inexplicable**, **lamentable**, **summarily**.

hostile HAHS-t<u>i</u>l.

The pronunciation HAHS-tyl (-tyl rhyming with *mile*) is British. See **textile**.

houses HOW-ziz, not HOW-siz or HOW-sis.

Houses is pronounced like *how's* and *is* strung together. In the singular *house* the S is pronounced like the S in *mouse,* but in the plural *houses* the middle S changes to a Z sound, as in *busy* and *rouse,* and the final, pluralizing S also is pronounced like Z, as in *boxes, churches, sentences*. This change from an S to a Z sound likewise occurs in the verb to *house* (HOWZ).

hovel HUHV-<u>u</u>l. Also, HAHV-<u>u</u>l. Do not say HOH-v<u>u</u>l.

Until the 1930s, dictionaries preferred the pronunciation HAHV-<u>u</u>l, in which the O has the sound of the O in *hot*. In the 1940s, Kenyon and Knott gave precedence to HUHV-<u>u</u>l, which rhymes with *shovel,* noting that HAHV-<u>u</u>l was much less frequently heard. Since then dictionaries have continued to list HAHV-<u>u</u>l, but HUHV-<u>u</u>l is universally preferred. See **grovel**.

huge HYOOJ. Do not say YOOJ. Pronounce the H. See **human**.

human HYOO-m<u>a</u>n. Do not say YOO-m<u>a</u>n. Pronounce the H. See **huge**.

hygienist hy-JEE-nist or HY-jee-nist.

For *hygienist* and the related word *hygienic,* current dictionaries recognize a number of different pronunciations. For *hygienist,* most have now settled on a preference for hy-JEE-nist, with the accent on the second syllable, which rhymes with *we*. HY-jee-nist, with the accent on the first syllable, is a shortened form of the older preferred pronunciation, HY-jee-uh-nist, with all four syllables articulated. The recent popular variant hy-JEN-ist (JEN- rhyming with *when*), appears in several current dictionaries but is not preferred.

For *hygienic,* the pronunciation HY-jee-**EN**-ik (four syllables, with the stress on the third) is listed first by all sources. Between the alternative pronunciations hy-JEE-nik and hy-JEN-ik it is a toss-up; older dictionaries tend to favor the former and recent ones the latter.

hysteria hi-STEER-ee-uh. Now often hi-STER-ee-uh.

Traditionally, this word is pronounced hi-STEER-ee-uh (STEER- rhyming with *fear*). In the last forty years, however, more and more people have begun to pronounce *hysteria* with the short E of *hysterical*: hi-STER-ee-uh. This pronunciation is now so popular that at least half of my current sources list it first.

The analogy with *hysterical* is false, for the words are divided differently, and this distinguishes them in pronunciation. *Hysterical* is divided *hys·ter·i·cal,* which makes the E in the *-ter-* syllable short, as in *sterile*. *Hysteria,* however, is divided *hys·te·ri·a*. Because the accented second syllable (-te-) ends in the vowel E, the E is long, as in *we*. Pronounced rapidly, the S blends with the T and the long E blends into the R; hence, hi-STEER-ee-uh. See **schizophrenia**, **wisteria**.

---

a = at • a̲ = woman • ah = spa • ahr = car • air = fair • ay = hay • aw = saw • ch = chip • e = let • e̲ = item • ee = see • eer = deer • i = sit • i̲ = direct • ng = sing • o̲ = connect • oh = go • oo = soon • or = for • oor = poor • ow = cow • oy = toy • sh = she • th = thin • t̲h̲ = them • u̲ = focus • uh = up • ur = turn • uu = pull, took • y, eye = by, pie • zh = measure

I

idea eye-DEE-uh. Do not say eye-DEER.

Idea has three syllables (*i·de·a*) and does *not* have an R at the end.

ignominy IG-no-MIN-ee, not ig-NAH-mi-nee.

Ignominy is accented on the first syllable (IG-), like *ig-norant* and *ignorance.* The mispronunciation ig-NAH-mi-nee, which shifts the stress to the second syllable so that the word rhymes with *hominy,* appears in *Webster* 3 (1961) and *Webster's Ninth* (1985) but is not recognized by other current dictionaries.

ignoramus IG-no-**RAY**-mus, not IG-no-**RAM**-us.

illustrative i-LUHS-truh-tiv, not **IL**-uh-STRAY-tiv.

Illustrative should be accented on the second syllable. The alternative **IL**-uh-STRAY-tiv, with the accent on the first syllable, has been recognized for about fifty or sixty years, but is not preferred.

impious IM-pee-us, not im-PY-us.

Don't be misled by the fact that *pious* is hidden in *impious.* The word is properly accented on the prefix *im-*, not on the *pi*. Say IM-pee-us.

impotent IM-puh-t<u>e</u>nt. Do not say im-POH-t<u>e</u>nt.

The mispronunciation im-POH-t<u>e</u>nt, with the accent on the second syllable, is relatively recent, and not recognized by most dictionaries. It is a tempting mispronunciation because the word *potent* is so apparent within *impotent,* so it is easy to imagine that the stress would fall on *po.* Not so. In *impotent* and *impotence,* the stress falls on the prefix *im-* (which means "not").

incognito Properly, in-KAHG-n<u>i</u>-toh. Now often IN-kahg-**NEE**-toh.

Incognito comes from the Latin *incognitus* (in-KAHG-ni-tuus), unknown, unrecognized, and should be stressed, like its root, on the second syllable (-cog-). Think of the word *cognitive* (KAHG-n<u>i</u>-tiv), or imagine how someone who travels *incognito* is as anonymous and unnoticed as a *cog* in a machine, and you will remember where the stress falls.

The variant IN-kahg-**NEE**-toh (with the stress on the penultimate syllable) was not recognized before the 1960s. *Webster* 3 lists IN-kahg-**NEE**-toh first, but at the same time marks it as unacceptable to many, giving in-KAHG-n<u>i</u>-toh as the less frequent but unobjectionable alternative.

IN-kahg-**NEE**-toh is still unacceptable to many—my mother, for instance, who caught me saying it a few years back and brought the issue to my attention. It is now so widely used, however, that many current authorities prefer it (including *Webster's Ninth, Webster's New World,* the *NBC Handbook,* and *Random House II*). Just as many, however, still do not: *American Heritage,* New College and Second College; *Funk & Wagnalls Standard*; and *Oxford American* all prefer in-KAHG-n<u>i</u>-toh, and *Scribner–Bantam* gives only this pronunciation.

increase (noun) IN-krees; (verb) in-KREES. See **decrease**.

inculcate Traditionally, in-KUHL-kayt. Now often IN-kul-kayt.

IN-kul-kayt, with the accent on the first syllable, was originally British. It has been used by educated American speakers for most of this century and is now standard. The traditional American pronunciation, which most current sources still prefer, retains the accent on the second syllable, in-KUHL-kayt. See **infiltrate**, **obfuscate**, **precedence**, **sonorous**.

indefatigable IN-di-**FAT**-i-guh-buul.

Indefatigable, which means incapable of being fatigued, untiring, is often mispronounced IN-di-fuh-TEEG-uh-buul, apparently by association with the verb *fatigue* (fuh-TEEG). The only pronunciation recognized by dictionaries, however, is IN-di-**FAT**-i-guh-buul, with the primary stress on **FAT**.

inexplicable in-EK-spli-kuh-buul.

Accent the *ex* in *inexplicable*. See **explicable**.

infiltrate Traditionally, in-FIL-trayt. Now often IN-fil-trayt.

The pronunciation IN-fil-trayt, with the accent on the first syllable, is a British import. It was not listed in American dictionaries before the 1960s, and is still not preferred by current American authorities. See **inculcate**, **obfuscate**, **precedence**, **sonorous**.

influence IN-floo-ents, not in-FLOO-ents.

Stress the *in* in *influence,* not the *flu*.

A growing number of educated speakers are shifting the accent in this word from the first syllable to the second, perhaps under the misapprehension that in-FLOO-ents is the more precise, or customary, or traditional American pronunciation. It is listed in only two of my sources, both Merriam-Webster dictionaries. *Webster* 3 (1961) says it is heard "sometimes" (see the Appendix for a discussion of this term as it is used in dictionaries), and *Webster's Ninth* (1985) labels it a southern regional pronunciation. Clearly, custom and authority place the accent on the first syllable, IN-floo-<u>e</u>nts, and the pronunciation in-FLOO-<u>e</u>nts, coming from anyone not born and raised in the southern United States, would appear to be an affectation.

inherent in-HEER-<u>e</u>nt (HEER- as in *hear* or *here*).

Pronounce the *here* in *in*here*nt*. It is popular today to say in-HER-<u>e</u>nt (with the short E sound of *herald*) or in-HAIR-<u>e</u>nt. These variants have been recognized for only about twenty-five years, and current dictionaries staunchly prefer in-HEER-<u>e</u>nt. In careful speech you still *hear* the *here* in *adhere* and *adherent* (ad-HEER-<u>e</u>nt), *cohere* and *co-herent* (koh-HEER-<u>e</u>nt), and *inhere* and *inherent* (in-HEER-<u>e</u>nt).

inhospitable in-HAHS-pit-uh-buul, not IN-hah-**SPIT**-uh-buul. See **hospitable**.

inquiry in-KWYR-ee. Also IN-kw<u>i</u>-ree.

The stress should be on the second syllable, as in the verb to *inquire*.

The pronunciation IN-kw<u>i</u>-ree, with the accent on the first instead of the second syllable, has been heard in educated speech for over a hundred years. A note in Worcester (1884) suggests that it may originally be a Scottish pronunciation. *Webster's New International* (1909) says it is "not recognized by orthoepists" but "sometimes used

---

a = at • <u>a</u> = woman • ah = spa • ahr = car • air = fair • ay = hay • aw = saw • ch = chip • e = let • <u>e</u> = item • ee = see • eer = deer • i = sit • <u>i</u> = direct • ng = sing • <u>o</u> = connect • oh = go • oo = soon • or = for • oor = poor • ow = cow • oy = toy • sh = she • th = thin • <u>th</u> = them • <u>u</u> = focus • uh = up • ur = turn • uu = pull, took • y, eye = by, pie • zh = measure

by good speakers." In the late 1920s and early 1930s, two influential dictionaries (*New Century* and *Webster 2*) recognized IN-kwi-ree, and since then it has been standard, though not preferred. Nearly all my current sources list in-KWYR-ee first.

integral IN-tuh-gral, not in-TEG-ral.

Integral should be accented on the first syllable, like *integer* and *integrate*. The variant in-TEG-ral, with the accent on the second syllable instead of the first, has been heard occasionally in educated speech since the early part of this century so that now most current dictionaries recognize in-TEG-ral but do not prefer it. IN-te-gral is by far the prevailing pronunciation, especially for the word's mathematical senses, and in-TEG-ral is still considered incorrect by many speakers. Also, be careful not to switch the G and R sounds in this word and say IN-truh-gal; this is nonstandard.

interest (noun) IN-trist; (verb) IN-trist or IN-tur-est. See **interesting**.

interesting IN-tur-es-ting or IN-tris-ting or **IN**-tur-ES-ting.

All three pronunciations are now standard, though not too long ago only the first was considered proper. (One reason there are so many accepted pronunciations is that most educated speakers do not say *interesting* in exactly the same way every time. Slight, unconscious variation is natural in rapid or informal speech, and when this occurs frequently and consistently with a certain word, it will usually become standard.)

There is one beastly mispronunciation of this word to avoid, however. Do not drop the first T and say **IN**-ur-ES-ting or **IN**-uh-RES-ting, as though the word were spelled *inneresting*. Dictionaries have not countenanced these pronunciations, and it is not likely that they will. See **interest**.

intravenous in-truh-VEE-n<u>u</u>s. Do not say in-truh-VEE-nee-<u>u</u>s.

Intravenous has four syllables, with the last two pronounced like the planet *Venus*. See **heinous**, **grievous**, **mischievous**.

irony EYE-ruh-nee. Do not say EYE-ur-nee.

The R in *irony* is not pronounced like the R in *iron*. It is pronounced like the R in *ironic*. The word should sound like a combination of the name *Ira* and the word *knee*.

irrelevant i-REL-uh-v<u>a</u>nt.

Be careful not to transpose the L and V sounds in this word and say i-REV-uh-l<u>a</u>nt, as though the word were spelled *irrevelant*. This is called metathesis—the transposition of a word's letters, syllables, or sounds; it occurs also in the nonstandard pronunciations NOO-kyuh-lur for **nuclear**, JOO-luh-ree for **jewelry**, and AKS for *ask*. Simply put, *metathesis* is a big word that means you are making a big mistake. See **cupola**, **diminution**, **February**, **jewelry**, **jubilant**, **nuclear**, **realtor**.

irreparable i-REP-uh-ruh-buul, not i-ruh-PAIR-uh-buul.

Irreparable does not incorporate the word *repair,* and should not be pronounced as if it does. Also, the word is divided *ir·rep·a·ra·ble* (not *ir·re·par·a·ble*), and this governs its pronunciation. There is a rare or obsolete word *irrepairable,* which was pronounced i-ruh-PAIR-uh-buul, but it is no longer listed in most dictionaries. The standard spelling today is *irreparable,* without the I, and the accent should be on the second syllable (-rep-). See **irrevocable**, **reparable**.

irrevocable i-REV-uh-kuh-buul, *not* i-ruh-VOH-kuh-buul.

Stress the second syllable (-rev-). Do not pronounce *irrevocable* as if it contained the verb to *revoke*. See **irreparable**.

Italian i-TAL-yin (initial I as in *sit.*)

The pronunciation eye-TAL-yin (with the initial I long, as in *site*) is a major no-no. *Random House II* says it "is heard primarily from uneducated speakers" and "is sometimes facetious or disparaging in purpose and is usually considered offensive."

J

jewelry JOO-wuul-ree. Do not say JOO-luh-ree.

To transpose the adjacent E and L in *jewelry,* pronouncing it JOO-luh-ree, as if it were spelled *jewlery,* is a major league beastly mispronunciation. This error may have been aggravated by the alternative spelling *jewellery,* which is British. To pronounce *jewelry* properly, say the word *jewel* and add *-ree*: JOO-wuul-ree. See **cupola**, **diminution**, **irrelevant**, **jubilant**, **nuclear**, **realtor**.

joust Traditionally, JUST. Now usually JOWST.

The *OED* says: "The historical English spelling from the 13th c. is *just*. . . . Under later French influence *joust* was used sometimes by Gower, Caxton, Spenser, and Milton, was preferred by Johnson, and used by Scott, and is now more frequent; but the pronunciation remained as in the historical spelling; the second pronunciation [JOOST] is recent, and suggested by the spelling *joust*."

The *OED* does not give the spelling pronunciation JOWST

---

a = at • a̲ = woman • ah = spa • ahr = car • air = fair • ay = hay • aw = saw • ch = chip • e = let • e̲ = item • ee = see • eer = deer • i = sit • i̲ = direct • ng = sing • o̲ = connect • oh = go • oo = soon • or = for • oor = poor • ow = cow • oy = toy • sh = she • th = thin • t̲h̲ = them • u̲ = focus • uh = up • ur = turn • uu = pull, took • y, eye = by, pie • zh = measure

(see Spelling Pronunciation in the Appendix), which is the most recent variant. In 1949, Kenyon and Knott listed JOWST after JUST, and in 1961 *Webster 3* gave JOWST precedence. Since then most authorities have followed suit, sometimes marking JUST as occasional or rare. However, the *NBC Handbook* (1984), which gives only one pronunciation for each entry, prefers JUST.

jubilant JOO-bi-lant.

Be careful not to say JOO-byoo-lant, as though the word were spelled *jubulant,* with two Us. See **cupola**, **diminution**, **irrelevant**, **jewelry**, **nuclear**, **realtor**.

junta Traditionally, JUHN-tuh. Now usually HUUN-tuh.

Junta has gone through a process called de-anglicization. This is when a foreign word that has been fully anglicized again takes on foreign characteristics, though not always ones it had formerly, and sometimes not even those of the language of origin.

"When the word *junta* was borrowed into English from Spanish in the early seventeenth century," explains *Random House II,* "its pronunciation was thoroughly Anglicized to [JUHN-tuh]. The twentieth century has seen the emergence and, especially in North America, the gradual predominance of the pronunciation [HUUN-tuh], derived from Spanish [HOON-tuh] through reassociation with the word's Spanish origins. A hybrid form [HUHN-tuh] is also heard."

This de-anglicized HUUN-tuh, which did not appear in dictionaries before the 1960s, is now preferred by most current authorities. The traditional, anglicized pronunciation JUHN-tuh is most often listed next, and sometimes dictionaries will give the original Spanish HOON-tuh. The hybrid HUHN-tuh, when it appears, is usually listed last. See **cadre**, **foyer**, **largess**, **lingerie**.

juror JOOR-ur, not JOOR-or.

The *-or* in *juror* should rhyme with *her,* not with *for.* This terminal *-or* comes from Latin and corresponds to the English *-er.* Both are noun endings, and in American speech both are properly pronounced UR. Thus the *-or* in *perpetrator, oppressor, protector, inventor,* and *prosecutor* (to name only a few of many such words) should sound the same as the *-er* in *doer* or *maker.*

Some speakers, however, insist on saying AK-tor for AK-tur, VEN-dor for VEN-dur, MEN-tor for MEN-tur, PRED-uh-tor for PRED-uh-tur, JOOR-or for JOOR-ur, and so on. These are overpronunciations, unnecessary exceptions imposed by those who try a bit too hard to sound exceptional. In *pastor, governor, conqueror, spectator, conductor, percolator,* and dozens more words, *-or* is properly sounded like *-er,* and there is no reason not to be consistent about it.

The inclination to exaggerate the pronunciation of certain words may come in part from a phenomenon of mass culture that I call "sci-fi pronunciation" or "Hollywood Technospeak." In American science-fiction movies and television shows, an alien standard of speech is commonly employed to heighten the illusion of otherworldliness. In the names of characters, fictitious places, and imaginary planets, the unstressed vowels are never lightened or elided as they would be in natural, conversational English, and the many androids, robots, and extraterrestrials we encounter tend either to affect a peculiar and inconsistent form of British accent or overpronounce each syllable in the manner of synthesized speech. Because these creatures appear to be free of the linguistic idiosyncrasies and intellectual imperfections of human beings (especially American ones), they can be intimidating as well as strange.

For example, in "Star Trek," Mr. Spock, the hyperarticulate character played by Leonard Nimoy, overpronounces the words *sensor, sector, factor,* and *record,* saying SEN-sor, SEK-tor, FAK-tor, and the British REK-ord instead of SEN-sur, SEK-tur, FAK-tur, and the American REK-urd. Spock, being Vulcan (and fictional to boot), can say whatever he likes, but we earthlings have our own standards to uphold. However, since it is the nature of Hollywood to sell, and because the overprecise speaker always touches a self-conscious nerve in us, Mr. Spock's and numerous other pseudo-precise sci-fi pronunciations have permeated American popular culture and been adopted by many otherwise unaffected speakers. Today their influence is particularly noticeable in the jargon (sometimes pronounced JAHR-gahn) of hi-tech, where *parameters* replace *perimeters,* the cognoscenti confer in acronyms, and a word processor becomes a word process-*or*. See **mentor**, **predator**, **vendor**.

juvenile Traditionally, JOO-ve-nil. Now also JOO-ve-nyl.

JOO-ve-nil (-nil like *-nal* in *annal*) is the standard American pronunciation; JOO-ve-nyl (-nyl rhyming with *pile*) is originally British. The latter is increasingly heard in America, especially for the noun, but the former is still preferred by American authorities. See **textile**.

K

kiln KIL or KILN.

KIL is the earlier standard; KILN is a spelling pronunciation that has been accepted for about sixty years and is now preferred by several dictionaries.

kismet KIZ-met or KIS-met.

Before the 1930s, dictionaries preferred KIS-met; since then they have switched their allegiance to KIZ-met, but continue to list KIS-met in good standing. Also acceptable, and preferred by some authorities, are the variants KIZ-m<u>e</u>t and KIS-m<u>e</u>t, in which the E is lightened so that it sounds like the E in *item*.

Koran k<u>o</u>-RAHN or k<u>o</u>-RAN.

Do not say KOR-an or KOH-ran, with the stress on the first syllable. The accent should be on the second syllable, which may sound like *Ron* or *ran*.

---

a = at • <u>a</u> = woman • ah = spa • ahr = car • air = fair • ay = hay • aw = saw • ch = chip • e = let • <u>e</u> = item • ee = see • eer = deer • i = sit • <u>i</u> = direct • ng = sing • <u>o</u> = connect • oh = go • oo = soon • or = for • oor = poor • ow = cow • oy = toy • sh = she • th = thin • <u>th</u> = them • <u>u</u> = focus • uh = up • ur = turn • uu = pull, took • y, eye = by, pie • zh = measure

L

lackadaisical LAK-uh-**DAY**-zi-kuul, not LAKS-uh-**DAY**-zi-kuul.

The odd mispronunciation *lax*-adaisical is heard from speakers not accustomed to listening to what they are saying. *Lackadaisical* connotes laxness, but it begins with *lack* and should be pronounced as it is spelled. The word comes from the archaic interjection *lackaday* (used to express sorrow, regret, or dismay), which in turn comes from *alackaday*.

lambaste lam-BAYST, not lam-BAST.

Thanks to my good friend James T. Mullin, a fine editor and speaker of the language, who lam-BAY-stid me for saying lam-BAST, I now know the preferred pronunciation.

lamentable LAM-en-ta-buul, not luh-MEN-ta-buul.

Lamentable should not be accented on the second syllable, like the verb to *lament*. *Lamentable, lament,* and *lamentation* are all accented differently. In *lamentation,* the primary stress is on the third syllable, LAM-en-**TAY**-shin; in *lament,* the stress is on the second syllable, luh-MENT; and in *lamentable,* the stress is properly on the first syllable, LAM-en-ta-buul.

Lamentable came into English from Latin in the fifteenth century. In the late sixteenth century, Spenser and Shakespeare placed the accent on the first syllable, and for the next three hundred years this was the only pronunciation sanctioned in cultivated speech. In the first half of the twentieth century, the pronunciation luh-MEN-ta-buul began to spread rapidly, though it went unrecognized by dictionaries and was severely criticized by many educated speakers.

In 1961, luh-MEN-ta-buul appeared in *Webster* 3, preceded by the symbol ÷, meaning it was unacceptable to many. This esoteric mark apparently eluded most readers, who could have benefited from a clearer warning that what followed was controversial. As a result, luh-MEN-ta-buul is now so widespread that the proper pronunciation almost seems old-fashioned. Yet, with only one exception (*American Heritage,* Second College) current sources remain steadfast in their preference for LAM-en-ta-buul. See **despicable**, **explicable**, **hospitable**, **inexplicable**, **summarily**.

largess Traditionally, LAHR-jis or LAHR-jes. Now usually lahr-JES or lahr-ZHES.

Largess dates back to the thirteenth century, and is related to the word *large*—which at one time meant generosity, bounty—as *riches* (formerly spelled *richesse*) is related to *rich*; hence, the traditional pronunciation with the accent on the first syllable. "If the word had remained in common use," writes Fowler, who prescribes the pronunciation LAHR-jis, "it would doubtless have come to be spelt, as it often formerly was, *larges*."

The *OED* shows that for several centuries the spellings *larges, largess,* and *largesse* were all in common use. By 1800, *larges* had begun to disappear. Today *largesse* is still used, but for the last hundred years dictionaries have preferred *largess,* with no E at the end.

The predominance of the double S spellings undoubtedly influenced the change in the pronunciation of this word. A reader encountering *largess* for the first time might easily assume the *-ess* is stressed, as in *caress, success,* and *redress.* To the speaker unfamiliar with the word's long history in English, the spelling *largesse,* with its final E, looks French, and would therefore seem to be pronounced like *finesse* and *noblesse.*

Until the middle of this century dictionaries recognized only LAR-jis and LAR-jes, but in the last thirty years most speakers have shifted the accent to the second syllable, and the traditional pronunciation, though still faithfully listed in current dictionaries, is infrequently heard. Today dictionaries prefer lahr-JES or lahr-ZHES, with a slight majority favoring the first. Regardless of where you choose to put the accent, the G should be pronounced like the G in *large,* as was customary for centuries. To give it a French ZH sound, as in *rouge,* is an illogical de-anglicization. For more on this term, see **cadre**, **junta**.

length LENGKTH. Do not say LENTH or LAYNTH.

Pronouncing *length* and *lengthen* as though they were spelled without the G is substandard, according to *Webster* 3—in other words, just above beastly, and definitely not the best. Current dictionaries all prefer LENGKTH. See **strength**.

liaison LEE-uh-zahn or LEE-ay-zahn or lee-AY-zahn or lee-ay-ZAW(N). Do not say LAY-uh-zahn.

Pronouncing the first syllable LAY is an improper anglicization, which is not recognized by some dictionaries, and never preferred.

LEE-uh-zahn and LEE-ay-zahn are the most frequently listed anglicized pronunciations. Closer to the French is lee-ay-ZAW(N), with a French nasal N and the accent on the final syllable; it is preferred by *Webster* 2 (1934) and *Random House II* (1987), and used by many cultivated speakers. Also acceptable, though less commonly heard, is lee-AY-zahn, with the accent on the second syllable.

library LY-brer-ee. Do not say LY-ber-ee or LY-buh-ree (as though the word were spelled *liberry*).

LY-brer-ee is universally preferred, and the most common pronunciation. LY-bruh-ree, though chiefly British, is also a standard variant among American speakers. Properly, *library* should have three syllables, but a two-syllable variant, LY-bree, occurs in educated speech and is listed in good standing in some current dictionaries.

The mispronunciation LY-ber-ee, according to *Webster's Ninth* (1985), is "heard from educated speakers, including college presidents and professors." If this is true, which I find hard to believe, I would seriously question the credentials of that president or professor and the institution he or she represents. Some well-educated people do speak poorly, but they are exceptions in an American system of higher education that, if it does little else, generally graduates students who speak standard English passably (writing it being another story). The note in *Random House II* (1987) seems closer to the truth: "[LY-ber-ee] is more likely to be heard from less educated or very young speakers, and is often criticized."

liege LEEJ. Do not say LEEZH. See **siege**.

---

a = at • a̱ = woman • ah = spa • ahr = car • air = fair • ay = hay • aw = saw • ch = chip • e = let • e̱ = item • ee = see • eer = deer • i = sit • i̱ = direct • ng = sing • o̱ = connect • oh = go • oo = soon • or = for • oor = poor • ow = cow • oy = toy • sh = she • th = thin • ṯẖ = them • u̱ = focus • uh = up • ur = turn • uu = pull, took • y, eye = by, pie • zh = measure

lingerie Properly, LAN-zhe-ree or lan-zhe-REE (lan- as in *land*). *Popularly, lahn-zhe-RAY, LAHN-zhe-ray; or lahn-je-RAY, LAHN-je-ray (lahn- as in longitude).*

Lingerie, which came into English from French in the nineteenth century, has been so mangled by English speakers that it is now almost impossible to pronounce it correctly and be understood. Words taken into English from other languages, if they occur frequently in speech, soon become anglicized in pronunciation. This is natural and appropriate. With *lingerie,* however, the process of anglicization has backfired and resulted in an inept and ludicrous imitation of the original French. The pronunciations popular today bear no resemblance to the French, nor do they sound English. It would be kind but inaccurate to call them anglicizations. They are best described as "manglicizations."

The French is lanzh-REE, and until about fifty years ago it was the only pronunciation countenanced in cultivated speech. Then all manner of permutations began to appear in the dictionaries. *Webster* 2 (1934) gives lanzh-REE, but adds, "popularly, LAHN-zhe-ree." Kenyon and Knott (1949) prefer LAN-zhe-ree, as does the *Winston Dictionary* (1951); the *American College* (1953), however, puts lahn-zhe-RAY first and LAN-zhe-ree second. Finally, *Webster* 3 (1961) covers all the bases by placing lahn-je-RAY at the head of a long series of variants followed by the admonition that vowels other than short A (as in *land*) in the first syllable and long E (as in *reed*) in the last syllable are regarded by many as substandard. So who said a dictionary was the place to go for a little straightforward advice?

In the 1959 film *Anatomy of a Murder,* in which a certain pair of panties figures prominently as evidence in a trial, Jimmy Stewart and George C. Scott both say lahn-zhe-ree, their stress varying from the first to third syllables. This pronunciation, recorded in *Webster* 2 (1934), still appears in most current dictionaries. Though it is a hybrid, it is preferable to the variants ending in -RAY because it at least properly anglicizes the final vowels -*ie* to conform with *reverie, coterie, bourgeoisie, jalousie,* and other analogous words.

My preferred pronunciations, LAN-zhe-ree and lan-zhe-REE, are the most faithful to the original vowel sounds of the French, and they are still listed in several current dictionaries. (One source—the *NBC Handbook*—prefers LAN-zhe-ree.) Unfortunately, they are now incomprehensible to most Americans. I offer them here, not with any false hope that they will catch on, only to bring to light a bit of bungled pretentiousness that somehow became the norm.

The funny thing about all this confusion is that *lingerie,* when you think about it, is a pretty silly word—a euphemism we have adopted to make something intimate and titillating sound innocuous at social gatherings and over department store loudspeakers. In *Anatomy of a Murder,* the judge asks counselors Stewart and Scott if there is an Anglo-Saxon word they can use in place of *lingerie* to make the testimony clearer and more specific. When Stewart slyly suggests "panties," the jury snickers, but the judge, realizing that panties are precisely what they are talking about, prudently lectures the jurors to keep their prurient connotations out of his courtroom. Since blank or puzzled faces usually meet my attempts to pronounce *lingerie* properly, and since I cannot bring myself to "manglicize" the word, these days, whenever I am about to utter it I say "women's underwear" instead—a plain English phrase that gets the point across just fine.

lithe LY_TH_ (TH as in *then*), not LYTH (TH as in *path*). *Lithe* should rhyme with *writhe*. See **blithe, loath**.

loath LOHTH (TH as in *both*). Do not say LOH<u>TH</u> (<u>TH</u> as in *bathe*).

Many experienced speakers—the television journalist and documentarian Bill Moyers, for example—fail to distinguish between the verb to *loathe,* to detest, abhor, and the adjective *loath,* unwilling, reluctant, disinclined.

The words are spelled and pronounced differently. The verb to *loathe,* because it has an E at the end, is pronounced LOH<u>TH</u>, with the "voiced" TH of *bathe, lathe,* and *lather.* The adjective *loath* has no final E, and so should be pronounced LOHTH, with a "voiceless" TH, to rhyme with *both* and *growth.* (The alternative spelling *loth,* which was common in the nineteenth century but has fallen out of use in this century, perhaps illustrates the proper pronunciation more clearly.) "When TH is final," explains *Webster* 2 (1934), "it is usually voiceless [with a few exceptions, such as smoo*th* and the verb to **bequea*th***]; when final and voiced, it is usually spelled *-the.*"

The verb to *loathe* is never mispronounced, but the adjective *loath* is so often mistakenly pronounced like the verb that the variant LOH<u>TH</u> for *loath* now appears in some current dictionaries. This is unfortunate, because the distinction in pronunciation between the verb and the adjective is a useful one, and it would be a shame to forfeit it out of ignorance. You may say that you *loathe* (LOH<u>TH</u>) doing something—detest doing it—but when you say you are *loath to* do something, take care to pronounce the word LOHTH, with the TH voiceless, as in *earth.* See **bequeath**, **blithe**.

loathsome LOH<u>TH</u>-sum, not LOHTH-sum.

Loathsome means causing *loathing* (LOH<u>TH</u>-ing), intense dislike or disgust. It should be pronounced like the verb to *loathe* plus *some,* but spelled without the terminal E of *loathe.* The misspelling *loathesome* is common but nonstandard. See **loath**.

long-lived LAWNG-LYVD, not LAWNG-LIVD.

The I in *long-lived* is long, as in *alive*.

Does *lived* in *long-lived* come from *life* or the verb to *live*? *Webster's New World Guide* (1984) says the pronunciation LIVD for *lived* "stems from the notion that the form (as in *long-lived*) comes from the verb *live,* but it is formed from the noun *life* plus the suffix *-ed*." Hence, the pronunciation LYVD, which is preferred by all my sources.

The popular but erroneous LAWNG-LIVD (with the short I of the verb to *live*) has been disparaged in dictionaries and pronunciation guides for most of this century. According to *Webster* 2 (1934), it may originally be an import from Britain. See **short-lived**.

---

a = at • a = woman • ah = spa • ahr = car • air = fair • ay = hay • aw = saw • ch = chip • e = let • e = item • ee = see • eer = deer • i = sit • i = direct • ng = sing • o = connect • oh = go • oo = soon • or = for • oor = poor • ow = cow • oy = toy • sh = she • th = thin • th = them • u = focus • uh = up • ur = turn • uu = pull, took • y, eye = by, pie • zh = measure

M

machination MAK-i-**NAY**-shin. Do not say MASH-i-**NAY**-shin.

The pronunciation MASH-i-**NAY**-shin appears in some current dictionaries, but it is not preferred. The CH in *machination* is pronounced like a K, not like SH—as in *Machiavelli*, not as in *machine*.

magi MAY-jy (MAY rhymes with *day*; -jy rhymes with *eye*).

The pronunciation MA-jy (MA- as in *mat*), which is sometimes heard, is not recognized by dictionaries. *Magi* is the plural of *magus* (MAY-gus).

maraschino MAR-uh-**SKEE**-noh, not MAR-uh-**SHEE**-noh.

The word *maraschino* is borrowed from Italian, and refers to an Italian sweet liqueur distilled from the juice of the *marasca* (muh-RAS-kuh), a bitter wild cherry. A *maraschino cherry* is one that has been preserved in or flavored with real or imitation *maraschino*. In Italian, the consonant blend SCH is pronounced like SK, as in the musical term *scherzo* (SKAIRT-soh), and this sound has been retained in the standard English pronunciation of *maraschino*. The variant MAR-uh-**SHEE**-noh, which is very often heard today, has appeared in dictionaries since the 1960s, but is not preferred.

mature muh-TUUR or muh-TYUUR or muh-TYOOR. Now also muh-CHUUR.

The pronunciation muh-TUUR (TUU as in *took*) has been standard for about forty years and preferred since the 1960s. The traditional pronunciation, still used by many cultivated speakers, is muh-TYOOR, with a long U or YOO sound, as in *cute*; in many current sources this has been modified to muh-TYUUR (YUUR as in *Europe*). Also common is muh-CHUUR, with the CH sound of *choose* replacing the T, as in *nature* and *picture*. Muh-CHUUR, which has been heard for several decades, was formerly considered substandard and is still sometimes criticized. However, though current sources do not prefer it, it has been listed since the 1960s and today is used by many educated speakers.

mauve MOHV, not MAWV.

Do not pronounce the AU in *mauve* like the AU in *Maude*. *Mauve* rhymes with *stove*.

mayoral MAY-ur-al. Do not say may-YOR-al.

Mayor, *mayoral*, and *mayoralty* all are accented on the first syllable: (may-).

The mispronunciations may-YOR-al, pas-TOR-al, pek-TOR-al, and EE-lek-**TOR**-al are increasingly heard, but are not recognized by dictionaries. *Mayoral*, *pastoral*, and *pectoral* have their accent on the first syllable; *electoral* is accented on the second. See **electoral**, **pastoral**, **pectoral**.

medieval MEE-dee-**EE**-val or MED-ee-**EE**-val.

Medieval should be pronounced in *four* syllables. Some current dictionaries list the three-syllable variants mee-DEE-val, med-EE-val, and mid-EE-val, which do not articulate the I in the second syllable. These relatively recent and unfortunately rather common corruptions are best avoided.

Medieval comes from the Latin *medius*, middle, and *aevum*, age, and is still sometimes spelled, as it was formerly, *mediaeval*. The pronunciations MEE-dee-**EE**-v<u>a</u>l (MEE- as in *meet*) and MED-ee-**EE**-v<u>a</u>l (MED- as in *medicine*) have both been in standard use for at least a century. American dictionaries universally prefer the former over the latter, which is originally British.

memento muh-MEN-toh. Do not say moh-MEN-toh.

The common mispronunciation moh-MEN-toh, with the long O of *mow* in the first syllable, arises from a confusion with such words as *moment* and *momentous*. *Memento*, a remembrance, keepsake, comes from a Latin word meaning remember. If you remember that *memento* begins with the *mem-* of re*mem*ber, you should have no trouble pronouncing or spelling it correctly.

memorabilia MEM-o-r<u>a</u>-**BIL**-ee-uh or MEM-<u>o</u>-r<u>a</u>-**BIL**-yuh. Do not say MEM-<u>o</u>-r<u>a</u>-**BEEL**-yuh (BEEL rhyming with *peel*).

The accented syllable in *memorabilia* (-bil-) should be pronounced like *bill*.

mentor MEN-tur. Now also MEN-tor.

Mentor, spelled with a capital, refers to the friend and adviser of Odysseus in Greek mythology. Spelled with a small letter, it means any wise and trusted counselor.

Several dictionaries now prefer the pronunciation MEN-tor, and it could be argued that this is more proper for the name (MEN-tor is the classical Greek pronunciation); however, this would necessitate making an awkward distinction between a Greek pronunciation for the name and an anglicized pronunciation for the English word that has developed from it.

No speaker I know makes this distinction, but many

use the Greek MEN-tor for both the word's senses. This can hardly be called wrong, for the pronunciation MEN-tor is recorded at least as far back as Worcester (1884); but it seems more sensible to accept the fully English MEN-tur, which is consistent with other English words ending in -*or*, and which is preferred by most older dictionaries and at least half of my current ones. See **juror**, **predator**, **vendor**.

merchandise (noun and verb) MUR-chan-dyz, not MUR-chan-dys.

Note the Z sound in the last syllable (-dise), which should rhyme with *size*; do not pronounce it like the word *dice*.

The suffix -*ise*, which takes its spelling from French, is equivalent to the suffix -*ize*, which comes from Greek. In *advertise*, *compromise*, *enterprise*, *improvise*, *exercise*, *supervise*, and *merchandise*, -*ise* is pronounced like -*ize*.

midwifery MID-wyf-ree or mid-WYF-ur-ee.

Contrary to popular belief, *midwifery* should be pronounced like *midwife* + -*ry*. This is the traditional American pronunciation, dating back at least to Noah Webster's dictionary of 1841, and preferred by the great *Century Dictionary* (1914), *Webster* 2 (1934), and *Webster* 3 (1961).

The pronunciations MID-wif-ree and mid-WIF-ur-ee (with the short I of *whiff*) are originally British, but were popular among American Anglophiles of the nineteenth century. Their recent resurrection in the United States has led many to believe they are correct; hence, three of my cur-

---

a = at • a̱ = woman • ah = spa • ahr = car • air = fair • ay = hay • aw = saw • ch = chip • e = let • e̱ = item • ee = see • eer = deer • i = sit • i̱ = direct • ng = sing • o̱ = connect • oh = go • oo = soon • or = for • oor = poor • ow = cow • oy = toy • sh = she • th = thin • t̲h̲ = them • u̱ = focus • uh = up • ur = turn • uu = pull, took • y, eye = by, pie • zh = measure

rent sources (*Webster's Ninth*, *Random House II*, and *Oxford American*) now list them first.

milieu meel-YUU.

Milieu's cluster of vowels makes it a particularly daunting word for English speakers to pronounce. Odd variations I have heard, some of which appear in recent dictionaries, include meel-YOO, MEEL-yoo, mil-YOO, MIL-yoo, mayl-YOO, and MAY-loo. All of these should be avoided.

Milieu comes from French and retains much of its foreign flavor in its pronunciation. The first syllable is pronounced meel-, like the word *meal*. (Also acceptable is mil-, like the first syllable of *million*.) The second syllable, which receives the accent, is pronounced like the *Eu-* in *Europe*: meel-YUU.

The plural may be spelled *milieus* or *milieux*, and may be pronounced either like the singular or with a Z sound at the end: meel-YUUZ. I recommend the terminal Z sound to distinguish the plural from the singular.

minuscule Properly, mi-NUHS-kyool. Now usually MIN-uh-skyool.

Minuscule comes from the Latin *minusculus* (mi-NUUHS-kuu-luus), smallish. As an adjective it may mean very small, or written in small or lower case letters as opposed to capital letters or *majuscule* (muh-JUHS-skyool); as a noun it may mean a small letter, or refer to a small, cursive style of ancient and medieval writing.

Minuscule is so often misspelled *miniscule*, as though it began with the prefix *mini-*, small, that three current sources—*Random House II*, *Webster's Ninth*, and *Webster 3*—recognize the misspelling as a legitimate variant. *Webster's New World* lists *miniscule* but marks it "erroneous," a label dictionary editors use—though not as freely as they once did, for times are more permissive—when a mistake is so common that they feel compelled to say, "Hey, we can't ignore the frequency of this in 'edited' writing, but why can't you folks out there get it right?"

(*Rarified* is another example of an erroneous spelling that has slipped by enough editors to be listed by some dictionaries as an acceptable variant for *rarefied*. *Rarified* probably caught on because it makes the word look as if it should be pronounced in three syllables—which it should—whereas *rarefied*, the proper spelling, could easily be misconstrued as being pronounced in two syllables.)

The misspelling *miniscule* has undoubtedly influenced the shift in the accent in *minuscule* from the second to the first syllable. The pronunciation MIN-uh-skyool does not appear in any of my sources before 1961, when *Webster* 3 gave it precedence. Since then only a handful of authorities have stuck by the traditional mi-NUHS-skyool, with the accent on the second syllable. (These include *Webster's New Twentieth Century* (1983), *Webster's New World Guide* (1984), and *Webster's New World* (1984), all published by Simon and Schuster.)

minutiae mi-NYOO-shee-ee or mi-NOO-shee-ee.

The *-ti-* is pronounced like the word *she*. (This same sound for *-ti-* occurs in **consortium**, **negotiate**, and *propitiate*.) The terminal AE is pronounced like double E in *need*. See **algae**, **consortium**, **negotiate**.

mischievous MIS-chi-vus. Stress the *first* syllable.

This word is subject to two beastly mispronunciations: mis-CHEE-vus and mis-CHEE-vee-us. The former is an archaism, and the latter, by metathesis, adds a nonexistent syllable to the word. Both place the accent on the wrong syllable.

The *OED* says, "The stressing on the second syllable

was common in literature till about 1700; it is now dialectal and vulgar." See **heinous**, **grievous**, **intravenous**.

mores Traditionally, MOH-reez or MOR-eez. Now usually MOR-ayz.

Mores, which entered English in 1898, means customs, folkways, and comes directly from the Latin plural of *mos* (MOHS), custom. At first it was pronounced MOH-reez (MOH- rhyming with *go*, -reez rhyming with *ease*), according to the rules for the so-called English pronunciation of Latin (see **data**).

By the 1940s, many speakers had softened the first syllable to sound like *more*, and the pronunciation MOR-eez appeared in the dictionaries. Then, twenty years later, the upstart MOR-ayz (-ayz rhyming with *maze*), without a prior appearance in a dictionary, arose and supplanted its predecessors.

A final variant, MOH-rays (-rays as in *race*), reflects the so-called Roman or classical pronunciation of Latin. It is not listed in most dictionaries but is still sometimes heard from disgruntled pedants who take exception to both MOR-ayz, which is now preferred, and MOR-eez, which is usually listed second.

N

naivete nah-eev-TAY (like *naive* + TAY).

With the words *naive* and *naivete* there is a tendency among many speakers to blend the A and I into a long I sound, which results in the pronunciations ny-EEV and ny-eev-TAY. These are so close to the proper pronunciations, nah-EEV and nah-eev-TAY, as to be nearly indistinguishable from them, and it would be almost pedantic to single them out as wrong. However, they appear in only one of my sources—*Webster* 3 (1961), which is particularly assiduous about recording variants. All others mark the A and I as having separate sounds. Therefore I suggest that if you can hear the distinction between nah- and ny- in the first syllable of *naive* and *naivete*, you should cultivate the preferred pronunciations: nah-EEV; nah-eev-TAY.

Now on to the serious mispronunciations to avoid. Do not say nah-EEV-uh-tay or nah-EEV-uh-tee (or ny-EEV-uh-tay and ny-EEV-uh-tee, for that matter). Standard word division allots *naivete* only three syllables: na·ive·te. Do

---

a = at • a̱ = woman • ah = spa • ahr = car • air = fair • ay = hay • aw = saw • ch = chip • e = let • e̱ = item • ee = see • eer = deer • i = sit • i̱ = direct • ng = sing • o̱ = connect • oh = go • oo = soon • or = for • oor = poor • ow = cow • oy = toy • sh = she • th = thin • ṯẖ = them • u̱ = focus • uh = up • ur = turn • uu = pull, took • y, eye = by, pie • zh = measure

---

not add a fourth in your pronunciation. You may stress the middle syllable (nah-EEV-tay), but the preferred pronunciation accents the final one (nah-eev-TAY), which should be pronounced TAY, never TEE.

nascent NAS-ent.

Many speakers may be surprised to learn that NAY-sent (NAY- rhyming with *say*), which is increasingly heard today in educated speech, is not the preferred pronunciation. (It apparently was shipped over from Great Britain, and has been listed as an alternative in American dictionaries since the 1930s.) The pronunciation NAS-ent (NAS- as in *nasty*) is preferred by thirteen out of sixteen current sources.

negotiate ne-GOH-shee-ayt, not ne-GOH-see-ayt.

Without a doubt, ne-GOH-see-ayt is the Great Beastly Mispronunciation of the 1980s, for it is in this decade that millions of speakers have suddenly decided to replace the traditional *shee* sound in this word with the oh-so-precious *see*. Much of the fault lies with the broadcast media, which all too often are in the vanguard of the vogue.

Broadcasters may be professional speakers, but most are no more knowledgeable about pronunciation than the next person. If you wouldn't take John or Jane Doe's word on how something should be pronounced, why take theirs? The next time you hear an unfamiliar pronunciation on TV or the radio, don't take it for granted that it's right—go to a dictionary (or two) and find out.

Case in point: The pronunciation ne-GOH-see-ayt does not appear in any of my sources. However, *Webster's Ninth* (1985) and *Random House II* (1987) now recognize ne-goh-see-AY-shin for *negotiation*, so I am sure it won't be long before ne-GOH-see-ayt makes its ignominious debut. Both are vogue pronunciations—fashionable and foppish, unwarranted and unnecessary. (See Vogue Pronunciation in the Appendix.) Also see **consortium**, **controversial**.

neither NEE-<u>th</u>ur. See **either**.

new Preferably, NYOO. Popularly, NOO.

In careful speech, *new* is pronounced NYOO, with a Y sound between the N and the OO. This is true also of words incorporating *new*: *newt*, *news*, *newscaster*, *newsletter*, *newlywed*, *newfangled*, and so on. See **dew**, **newspaper**.

newspaper NYOOZ-pay-pur or NOOZ-pay-pur.

The S has a Z sound. Do not say NOOS-pay-pur.

nihilism NY-i̠-liz-u̠m (NY- rhymes with *high*).

NY-i̠-liz-u̠m is preferred by all my current sources. The variant NEE-i̠-liz-u̠m (NEE- as in *need*), which was first recorded in the 1960s, is often listed second. It seems to be modeled after the classical Latin pronunciation of the root word of *nihilism*: *nihil*, nothing. In classical Latin, *nihil* is pronounced NI-hil, not NEE-hil. (According to the system for the English pronunciation of Latin, *nihil* is pronounced NY-hil.)

Classical Latin pronunciations (especially *incorrect* ones) for established, anglicized English words are at best eccentricities and at worst vogue pronunciations. (See the Appendix and **consortium**, **controversial**, **negotiate** for more on vogue pronunciations.) For NI-hil-iz-u̠m there would be some remote authority; NEE-i̠-liz-u̠m, however, has nothing to recommend it other than its dubious current popularity.

The *nihil* in *nihilism* and *annihilate* should be pronounced with the initial I long, as in *nice*, and the H silent. Formerly it was proper to pronounce the H in both words, but since the 1930s it has almost entirely disappeared from cultivated speech. Today *nihilism* with the H sounded still appears in some dictionaries, but the H sound in *anni-hilate* has not been recorded for about thirty years.

nuclear NYOO-klee-ur or NOO-klee-ur. Do not say NOO-kyuh-lur.

In his introduction to the fourth edition of the *NBC Handbook of Pronunciation* (1984), veteran broadcaster and language commentator Edwin Newman remarks that when the *nuclear* age began in August 1945, so did the "*nucular* age" as well.

Ever since *nuclear* entered the national vocabulary (a hundred years after entering English in the 1840s) it has been mispronounced by millions of educated and otherwise careful speakers, including scientists, lawyers, professors, and presidents of the United States. According to Newman, Dwight D. Eisenhower "could not get it right"; Jimmy Carter, who had been an officer aboard *nuclear*-powered submarines, pronounced it NOO-kee-ur; and Walter Mondale, in his 1984 campaign for the presidency, repeatedly said "nucular." "The word, correctly pronounced," writes Newman, "somehow is too much for a fair part of the population, and education and experience seem to have nothing to do with it."

This rather cynical conclusion reminds me of a debate I once heard between William F. Buckley and the philosopher Mortimer Adler on whether everyone is inherently "educable," or whether some people, by nature or by circumstance, are "ineducable." (Of course, Buckley, who earns his living trying to make his ideological opponents look hopelessly dull and impervious to illumination, was of the latter opinion.) I choose to believe that anyone in possession of physiologically normal organs of speech is capable of pronouncing *nuclear* correctly. The error is one of the ear more than the tongue, and it has persisted not because it is impossible for some to say NYOO-klee-ur or NOO-klee-ur, but because they do not hear the difference between the proper and improper pronunciations—which brings us to the matter of correction.

Those who do hear the mispronunciation and who say the word right (still a large majority of us) are understandably reluctant to correct those who do not. Can you imagine, as Edwin Newman puts it, "how other and lesser members of the Carter administration found it tactful to pronounce [*nuclear*] during Cabinet meetings," when President Carter and Vice President Mondale were mangling the word, albeit unwittingly, at every turn? In Shaw's *Pygmalion*, the arrogant dialectician, Henry Higgins, "experiments" without the slightest compunction on his social inferior, Liza Doolittle, the "guttersnipe," teaching her to speak Received Standard English so he can win a bet. But what American feels comfortable correcting the pronunciation of anyone but a child without being asked to do so? It is a tricky business even to correct family members and friends, and so with a neighbor, acquaintance, or business associate, most of us will not—and *should* not—presume to offer an unsolicited opinion.*

On the other hand, we should and do reserve the right,

---

*Let me point out here that writing a book on the subject is a different issue, for a book lays open its opinions only to those who freely choose to read it, and who are equally free to accept or reject the advice it contains without compromising their dignity.

---

a = at • a̲ = woman • ah = spa • ahr = car • air = fair • ay = hay • aw = saw • ch = chip • e = let • e̲ = item • ee = see • eer = deer • i = sit • i̲ = direct • ng = sing • o̲ = connect • oh = go • oo = soon • or = for • oor = poor • ow = cow • oy = toy • sh = she • th = thin • t̲h̲ = them • u̲ = focus • uh = up • ur = turn • uu = pull, took • y, eye = by, pie • zh = measure

in matters of language, to speak as we see fit and pass tacit judgment on our peers. When I began writing this book, nearly every person with whom I discussed its contents asked (and in some cases implored) me to decry NOO-kyuh-lur, which made me wonder whether it might be the Most Recognized Beastly Mispronunciation in the language. *Webster's Ninth* (1985) and *Random House II* (1987) both say that NOO-kyuh-lur is "disapproved of by many," but by just how many it is impossible to determine. On behalf of the indeterminate many who pronounce the word correctly, then, I appeal to the inadvertent many who do not: Listen, and be errant no longer.

Molecular comes from *molecule*, and *particular* comes from *particle*, but there is no "nucule" to support "nucular." *Nuclear* comes from *nucleus* (NYOO-klee-us or NOO-klee-us), which is almost never mispronounced. If you can say *nucleus* and you can say *nuke*—the informal word for *nuclear*—then the proper pronunciation of *nuclear* is but a suffix away. (See **gondola** for more on correcting others' pronunciation.) See **cupola**, **diminution**, **February**, **irrelevant**, **jewelry**, **jubilant**, **realtor**.

nuptial NUHP-shuul.

NUHP- rhymes with *cup*; -shuul rhymes with *full*.

NUHP-shuul is the preferred pronunciation; the alternative NUHP-chuul, which is about fifty years old, appears in most current dictionaries.

Nuptial has two syllables. Do not say NUHP-shoo-al or NUHP-choo-al. According to most authorities, these three-syllable variants are "unacceptable to many" or "substandard," designations that in this book translate to "beastly." (See Substandard in the Appendix.)

O

obeisance oh-BAY-sans or oh-BEE-sans.

The last syllable, (-sance), is pronounced like the word *since*, not like the word *sins*.

Obeisance, which dates back to the fourteenth century, is a venerable literary word for a deferential gesture, such as a bow, curtsy, or genuflection. The accent falls on the second syllable (-bei-) in *obeisance*, which you may pronounce either with the sound of long A (BAY) or long E (BEE). Both these pronunciations have been in cultivated use in America and England since the late eighteenth century. However, if you are not already accustomed to using one or the other, it may be helpful to bear in mind that the preponderance of authority in both the past and present centuries favors oh-BAY-sans. Out of twenty-five twentieth-century sources polled, only four prefer oh-BEE-sans.

obelisk AHB-uh-lisk. Do not say OH-buh-lisk.

The *ob-* in *obelisk* should be pronounced like *ob-* in the noun *object* or the verb *obligate*. *Obelisk* is divided ob·e·lisk, which gives the O (because it combines with B to form the first syllable) the AH sound of the O in *hot*. If the word were divided o·be·lisk, with just O in the first syllable, the O would have the long sound of *go*. The pronunciation OH-buh-lisk, with the long O, appears as a variant in two current dictionaries, but is not recognized by any of my other sources.

obfuscate ahb-FUHS-kayt or AHB-fus-kayt.

The traditional American pronunciation is ahb-FUHS-kayt, with the accent on the second syllable; AHB-fus-kayt, with the first syllable accented, is British. AHB-fus-kayt has been heard in educated American speech since the early part of this century, but went unrecognized by American dictionaries and was criticized by the prominent American orthoepists W. H. P. Phyfe (in *18,000 Words Often Mispronounced*, 1926) and Frank H. Vizetelly (in *Desk-Book of Twenty-Five Thousand Words Frequently Mispronounced*, 1929).

Despite all authoritative injunctions, the American homegrown flavor of ahb-FUHS-kayt was soon overwhelmed by the peculiar aroma of sophistication and *savoir-vivre* that emanated from the British AHB-fus-kayt. The import first appeared in American dictionaries in the 1930s, and since the 1960s has been preferred by most of them. See **inculcate**, **infiltrate**, **precedence**, **sonorous**.

oblique uh-BLEEK.

Though some dictionaries now prefer it, the pronunciation oh-BLEEK (oh- rhyming with *go*) is incorrect. Because the first syllable is unstressed, the quantity of the O is neither short (AH as in *opt*) or long (OH as in *pope*) but lightened to sound like the initial O in *oppose*, *oblige*, *obscure*, or the verb to *object*.

The pronunciation uh-BLYK (-BLYK rhyming with *like*), which enjoyed its heyday in the nineteenth century, is still common in military usage. See **official**.

official uh-FISH-ul. Do not say oh-FISH-ul.

Some speakers think it sounds more uh-FISH-ul to say oh-FISH-ul, with the initial O long, as in *snow*. This is an overpronunciation. Modern phoneticians call the initial vowel sound in this word a *schwa*; dictionary makers of a hundred years ago called it "obscure." All this means is that the first syllable of *official*, because it is unstressed, is pronounced like the A in *ago*, not like the O in *open*.

often AWF-en or AHF-en. Do not say AWF-ten or AHF-ten.

"The sounding of the T," writes H. W. Fowler in *Modern English Usage* (1926), "is practised by two oddly consorted classes—the academic speakers who affect a more precise enunciation than their neighbours . . . and the uneasy half-literates who like to prove that they can spell."

Webster 2 (1934), which gives only AWF-en, notes that "the pronunciation [AWF-ten], until recently generally considered as more or less illiterate, is not uncommon among the educated in some sections, and is often used in singing."

According to *Random House II* (1987):

> OFTEN was pronounced with a t- sound until the 17th century, when a pronunciation without (t) came to pre-dominate in the speech of the educated, in both North America and Great Britain, and the earlier pronunciation fell into disfavor. Common use of a spelling pronunciation has since restored the (t) for many speakers, and today [AWF-en] and [AWF-ten] . . . exist side by side. Although it

---

a = at • a = woman • ah = spa • ahr = car • air = fair • ay = hay • aw = saw • ch = chip • e = let • e = item • ee = see • eer = deer • i = sit • i = direct • ng = sing • o = connect • oh = go • oo = soon • or = for • oor = poor • ow = cow • oy = toy • sh = she • th = thin • th = them • u = focus • uh = up • ur = turn • uu = pull, took • y, eye = by, pie • zh = measure

is still sometimes criticized, **OFTEN** with a (t) is now so widely heard from educated speakers that it has become fully standard once again.

I would caution those who might be consoled by these last remarks to heed the admonitions of the past and avoid pronouncing the T. Current dictionaries, including *Random House II*, do not prefer AWF-t<u>e</u>n, and it is much less common in educated speech and far more often criticized by cultivated speakers—particularly teachers of speech, drama, and elocution—than *Random House II* makes it appear. In 1932, the English lexicographer Henry Cecil Wyld called the pronunciation AWF-t<u>e</u>n "sham-refined," and today the bad odor of class-conscious affectation still clings to it as persistently as ever. As if that were not enough, analogy is entirely unsupportive: No one pronounces the T in *soften, listen, fasten, moisten, hasten, chasten, christen,* or *Christmas*—so, once and for all, let's do away with the eccentric AWF-t<u>e</u>n.

olfactory ahl-FAK-tur-ee, not ohl-FAK-tur-ee.

The *ol-* should be pronounced like the *ol-* in *Oliver*. The pronunciation ohl-FAK-tur-ee (ohl- rhyming with *hole*) has been listed in dictionaries for about twenty years, but is not preferred by any of my current sources.

oligarchy **AHL**-<u>i</u>-GAHR-kee, not **OH**-l<u>i</u>-GAHR-kee.

Oligarchy means literally "government by the few," and very few members of the current oligarchy of lexicographers and orthoepists recognize the pronunciation **OH**-l<u>i</u>-GAHR-kee, with the long O of *no*. Pronounce the *ol-* in *oligarchy* like the *ol-* in *olive* or *olfactory*. See **olfactory**.

onerous AHN-ur-<u>us</u>, not OHN-ur-<u>us</u>.

Though *onerous*, burdensome, and *onus*, a burden, are related etymologically, they have different pronunciations.

The initial O in *onus*, which is divided o·nus, is long, as in *bone*: OH-nus. The initial O in *onerous*, which is divided on·er·ous, has the short sound of *on*: AHN-ur-us.

onomatopoeia AHN-o-MAT-o-**PEE**-uh.

Note the T in the third syllable (-mat-) of *onomatopoeia*, and take care to pronounce it clearly. Do not replace the T with an N and say AHN-o-MAHN-o-**PEE**-uh.

ophthalmologist AHF-thal-**MAHL**-uh-jist.

In *ophthalmologist* and *ophthalmology*, the PH is pronounced like an F. Do not say AHP-thal-**MAHL**-uh-jist. See **diphtheria**, **diphthong**.

orthoepy **OR**-thoh-EP-ee or or-THOH-i-pee or OR-thoh-i-pee or or-THOH-uh-pee.

These are all standard American pronunciations. The first is my preference. See Orthoepist, Orthoepy in the Appendix for a further discussion of this word's origin, meaning, and the imbroglio over its pronunciation.

P

paean PEE-an. Do not say PAY-an.

PEE-an is the only recognized pronunciation for this word, which means a song or hymn of praise.

palm PAHM. Do not say PAHLM. The L is silent. See **calm**.

paradigm PAR-uh-dim or PAR-uh-dym.

This is one of the many strange-looking English words that make the language such a beastly one to learn to pronounce properly. In *paradigm*, the odd placement of a G before an M poses a problem—is it sounded, and if so, how? The answer is the G is left over from the Latin and Greek forms of the word, and, like those languages, is dead, unspoken. In the noun *paradigm*, an example, model, or pattern, the G is silent; but in the adjective *paradigmatic*, the G is pronounced: PAR-uh-dig-**MAT**-ik.

Then there is the matter of the I in -digm: Is it short or long? PAR-uh-dim (-dim like *dim*) is the traditional American pronunciation, the only one given by Worcester (1884) and the *Century* (1914). PAR-uh-dym (-dym like *dime*), which has been listed in American dictionaries since the early 1900s, is originally British.

It is an odd consequence of the historical relationship between Great Britain and the United States and of our respective national characters that, in spite of the international dominance of American English in the twentieth century, American pronunciations are rarely adopted by the British but numerous British pronunciations have caught on in America. Why is this the case, and not the other way around? Could it be that Americans have never quite gotten over believing that English somehow belongs to England, and our brand of it will forever be a corruption of the mother tongue? This may be the sentiment of "a formidable sect of Anglomaniacs," as H. L. Mencken puts it, but most Americans, he asserts in *The American Language* (4th ed. 1937), "believe that their way of using English is clearly better than the English way." Perhaps, then, it is the British who have advanced this notion by taking every opportunity to show contempt for American vocabulary, idioms, accent, and literature (Mencken documents this scrupulously), and to invent pronunciations that call attention to the presumed superiority of their style of speech.

I doubt whether many take this conflict between what Mencken calls "the two streams of English" very seriously anymore, yet for much of our history it was a lively and thoroughly malicious one, filled with sarcasm and punctuated by fulminations from both sides. The origin of the controversy goes back, of course, to the War of Independence. In his *Dissertations on the English Language* (1789), Noah Webster reminds the citizens of the new republic that the Revolution was fought for linguistic as well as political freedom. "As an independent nation," he writes, "our honor requires us to have a system of our own, in language as well as government. Great Britain,

---

a = at • a̲ = woman • ah = spa • ahr = car • air = fair • ay = hay • aw = saw • ch = chip • e = let • e̲ = item • ee = see • eer = deer • i = sit • i̲ = direct • ng = sing • o̲ = connect • oh = go • oo = soon • or = for • oor = poor • ow = cow • oy = toy • sh = she • th = thin • t̲h̲ = them • u̲ = focus • uh = up • ur = turn • uu = pull, took • y, eye = by, pie • zh = measure

whose children we are, and whose language we speak, should no longer be *our* standard; for the taste of her writers is already corrupted, and her language on the decline."

Though we won our political freedom from England, and the hot debate over whose English is the best has dwindled to a rather uneventful cold war, the struggle nevertheless goes on, and with *paradigm* the British seem to have scored another victory. Until the 1960s, American dictionaries preferred PAR-uh-dim. Since then their preference has been about equally divided between -dim and -dym. Today, claims *Webster's New World Guide* (1984), "fewer and fewer people are saying PAR-uh-dim." Though the future looks grim for PAR-uh-dim, I don't give a dime for PAR-uh-dym, and folks, I have not yet begun to fight. United we stand, divided we fall. *Paradigm* is *e pluribus unum*, one out of many. I regret that I have only one life to lose for my country, but I say give me PAR-uh-dim or give me death!

parley PAHR-lee, not PAHR-lay.

Parley and *parlay* have different meanings, spellings, and pronunciations. A *parley* is a conference, especially with an enemy. A *parlay* is a bet in which the original stake plus its winnings are wagered again or successively. *Parlay*, the bet, ends in *-lay* and is pronounced PAHR-lay (-lay rhyming with *day*). *Parley*, the conference, ends in *-ley* and is pronounced PAHR-lee (-lee rhyming with *see*).

pastoral PAS-tuh-ral. Do not say pas-TOR-al.

In *pastor* and *pastoral*, *pasture* and *pastural*, the accent is on the first syllable. See **electoral**, **mayoral**, **pectoral**.

pectoral PEK-tuh-ral. Do not say pek-TOR-al.

Stress the *pec-* in *pectoral*, not the *-tor-*. See **electoral**, **mayoral**, **pastoral**.

penalize PEE-nuh-lyz, not PEN-uh-lyz.

The verb to *penalize*, which entered the language in the 1860s, is pronounced PEE-nuh-lyz (PEE- like *pea*) because it is formed from the adjective *penal* (PEE-n<u>a</u>l) plus the suffix *-ize*. The alternative PEN-uh-lyz, which is based on false analogy with *penalty* (PEN-<u>a</u>l-tee), has been recorded in dictionaries since the 1940s but is not preferred.

permit (noun) PUR-mit; (verb) pur-MIT.

Do not say pur-MIT for both noun and verb. The noun *permit* is accented on the first syllable (PUR-mit), and the verb to *permit* is accented on the second (pur-MIT). See **decrease**, **transfer**.

phenomenon fuh-NAHM-uh-nahn.

Pronounce the ending -non in *phenomenon* like the prefix *non-* in *nonsense*. The variant fuh-NAHM-uh-n<u>u</u>n, in which -non sounds like the word *none*, is originally British.

pianist pee-AN-ist, not PEE-uh-nist.

It has been my experience that those who say PEE-uh-nist seem quite sure that those who say pee-AN-ist are wrong, whereas those who say pee-AN-ist tend to wonder whether those who say PEE-uh-nist are putting on the dog.

The answer is that for nearly a hundred years American dictionaries have listed PEE-uh-nist, with the accent on the first syllable, but preferred pee-AN-ist, with the accent on the second syllable (like *piano*), for the latter has always been the more common of the two pronunciations in educated speech on this side of the Atlantic. PEE-uh-nist is preferred by the *OED* and several other British authorities from the first half of this century, and may ultimately be British in origin—though Worcester's dictionary (1884), which prefers pee-AH-nist with the Italian A, notes that Noah Webster (1841) gives PY-uh-nist (PYlike *pie*), a rather eccentric pronunciation that nevertheless shows an early recessive accent in American speech. What this boils down to is that if you say PEE-uh-nist, you are not being "more correct," only a bit different and a tad more British. On the other hand, if you say pee-AN-ist, you won't need a tuxedo to play along with anyone.

piquant PEE-kint.

This is the universally preferred pronunciation.

Piquant is an old word. It came into English in the early seventeenth century from the French *piquer*, to prick, sting, goad, the source also of the English verb to *pique* (PEEK). The preferred pronunciation, which has been established for well over a hundred years, retains the French EE sound for the I and the French K sound for the QU, but anglicizes the accent, placing it on the first syllable, which obscures the A in the second syllable: PEE-kint.

An acceptable alternative is PEE-kahnt (-kahnt rhyming with *want*), which usually appears second in most current dictionaries. A third variant, pee-KAHNT, is undesirable because it shifts the traditional accent from the first to the second syllable. Other recent variants include PEE-kant, pee-KANT, PEE-kwunt, PEE-kwahnt, and the increasingly common but erroneous PIK-wunt. All of these are best avoided. Say PEE-kint: Dictionaries overwhelmingly favor it, and it is neither pretentious nor difficult to pronounce.

plantain PLAN-tin. Do not say PLAN-tayn.

Dictionaries do not recognize the spelling pronunciation PLAN-tayn (-tayn rhyming with *cane*). The -tain in *plantain* is pronounced like the -tain in *captain*, and the word should sound like a combination of *plan* and *tin*. (See Spelling Pronunciation in the Appendix.)

poinsettia poyn-SET-ee-uh.

This hardy, colorful plant is named after the American diplomat J. R. Poinsett (1799–1851), who brought it from Mexico to the United States in 1828. There are two things to remember about pronouncing *poinsettia* properly: (1) it has four syllables (do not say poyn-SET-uh); and (2) it does not begin with the word *point* (do not say *point-settia*).

porcupine POR-kyuh-pyn.

The pronunciation POR-kee-pyn (like *porky* + *pine*) is not recognized by dictionaries. In children it can be endearing, but not in adults. Pronounce the -cu- in *porcupine* like -cu- in *occupy*.

possess puh-ZES. Do not say poh-ZES. See **official**.

precedence pri-SEED-ens or, usually, PRES-uh-dens.

Precedence came into English in the late fifteenth century, and its current sense of priority, the right to come before, originated about 1600. Samuel Johnson's dictionary of 1755, one of the first to give pronunciation, shows the accent on the second syllable (pri-SEED-ens), and quotes verses from Shakespeare, Milton, and Dryden to illustrate it.

The pronunciation PRES-uh-dens, with the accent on the first syllable, began to gain currency sometime in the early nineteenth century. Though denounced as erroneous by Worcester (1884), and ignored by the *Century* (1914), the *OED* (completed in 1928), and *Webster* 2 (1934),

---

a = at • a = woman • ah = spa • ahr = car • air = fair • ay = hay •
aw = saw • ch = chip • e = let • e = item • ee = see • eer = deer
• i = sit • i = direct • ng = sing • o = connect • oh = go • oo =
soon • or = for • oor = poor • ow = cow • oy = toy • sh = she •
th = thin • th = them • u = focus • uh = up • ur = turn • uu =
pull, took • y, eye = by, pie • zh = measure

by the 1920s PRES-uh-dens had become so prevalent in educated speech (in Great Britain, at any rate) that H. W. Fowler declared in *Modern English Usage* that the lexicographic community's disdain for pri-SEED-ens was "a very disputable account of present usage." Fowler then recommended PRES-uh-dens "for all alike" on the assumption that it would prevail.

Though Fowler's prediction was correct, it was not until the 1940s that PRES-uh-dens was recognized by dictionaries, and it did not gain pri-SEED-ens or PRES-uh-dens until 1961. Even then, *Webster* 3, the first to put PRES-uh-dens first, was not entirely confident about its standing, and so preceded it with the symbol ÷, meaning it was still unacceptable to many. Today, however, the verdict is clear: PRES-uh-dens, the British innovation, is preferred, and pri-SEED-ens, the traditional pronunciation, though listed in good standing by all current sources—and preferred by the *NBC Handbook* (1984)—is far less frequently heard. See **inculcate**, **infiltrate**, **obfuscate**, **paradigm**, **sonorous**.

predator PRED-uh-tur, not PRED-uh-tor.

The terminal -or is pronounced like -er (UR). See **juror**, **mentor, vendor**.

preferable PREF-ur-uh-buul, not pruh-FUR-uh-buul.

Despite what you may have heard from the Great Communicator, Ronald Reagan, *preferable* and *prefer* have different accents. *Prefer* is accented on the second syllable; *preferable* is accented on the first syllable, like *preference*. See **admirable**, **comparable**, **irreparable**, **irrevocable**.

prelude PREL-yood. Do not say PRAY-lood.

The pronunciation PRAY-lood has recently caught on to the point where most current dictionaries now include it as an alternative to the preferred pronunciation, PREL-yood. Despite its similarity to the French, PRAY-lood is an affectation—a de-anglicization—for the word has long been anglicized (it came into English in the sixteenth century). Suddenly to say PRAY-lood after hundreds of happy years saying PREL-yood is like one day deciding to say BLAWNSH for *blanch*, or roh-mawn-TEEK for *romantic*. I say let's leave PRAY-lood where it probably began—with that peculiar clan of pseudo-sophisticated voice-overs who sell cheap wine, cars, and low-cal TV dinners. (For more on anglicization and de-anglicization, see **cadre**, **foyer**, **junta**, **largess**, and **lingerie**.)

premises PREM-i-siz, not PREM-i-seez. See **process**.

premonition pree-muh-NISH-un, not prem-uh-NISH-un.

Premonition came into English from Latin in the fifteenth century. The pronunciation prem-uh-NISH-un (prem- as in *premise*) has appeared in dictionaries since the 1960s. Out of ten current sources polled, nine prefer pree-muh-NISH-un (pree- as in *premium*).

preparatory pri-PAR-uh-tor-ee, not PREP-uh-ruh-tor-ee.

Preparatory has five syllables, and the accent should fall on the second (-par-), in which the A has the sound of the A in *parent*. The pronunciation PREP-uh-ruh-tor-ee, with the accent on the first syllable, has been listed since the 1960s, but is not preferred by any current sources. A four-syllable variant, PREP-ruh-tor-ee, is marked "unacceptable to many" by *Webster* 3 (1961).

prestigious pre-STIJ-us, not pre-STEE-jus.

For *prestige*, the pronunciation pre-STEEZH is universally preferred, with pre-STEEJ listed as the alternative in current dictionaries. For *prestigious*, nine out of ten current sources prefer pre-STIJ-us. See **capricious**.

primer (book of elementary principles) PRIM-ur.

The British pronunciation is PRY-mur.

privilege PRIV-uh-lij, not PRIV-lij.

Careful speakers pronounce the word in three syllables.

process PRAH-ses. PROH-ses is British.

N.B.: The plural *processes* is pronounced PRAH-ses-iz, with the terminal -es pronounced -iz, as in *kisses* or *excuses*. Do not say PRAH-ses-seez. See **premises**, **processor**.

processor PRAH-ses-ur, not PRAH-ses-or. See **juror**.

program PROH-gram, not PROH-grum.

"Do not slur over the *a* in the second syllable," counsels John G. Gilmartin in *Everyday Errors in Pronunciation* (1936). "You do not say *telegr'm*—do not say *progr'm*. The *gram* should be clearly pronounced."

One need only compare the sound of -gram in *cablegram, anagram, cryptogram, kilogram, milligram, monogram,* and *diagram* to see that Gilmartin's advice is sound.

progress PRAH-gres. PROH-gres is British. See **process**.

promulgate Traditionally, pruh-MUHL-gayt or proh-MUHL-gayt. Now usually PRAH-mul-gayt.

The pronunciation PRAH-mul-gayt, with the accent on the first syllable, is originally British (along with PROH-mul-gayt, which flopped in America). After its appearance in the *OED* (c. 1928), American dictionaries began to include it, usually with the notation "especially British." That didn't scare anyone, however, and by the 1960s PRAH-mul-gayt had become especially American as well. Of the seventeen post-1960s sources I surveyed, only two prefer the accent on the second syllable. Nearly all, however, list pruh-MUHL-gayt or proh-MUHL-gayt as alternatives, and there are still a fair number of undaunted speakers (William F. Buckley is one prominent example) who put the stress in *promulgate* on -mul- rather than prom-. Whether they do so out of habit, or pride, or an obstinate brand of patriotism (my reason), I cannot say. See **inculcate**, **infiltrate**, **obfuscate**, **paradigm**, **precedence**, **sonorous**.

pronunciation pro̱-NUHN-see-**AY**-shi̱n.

Many who claim to be careful speakers boast of their good pruh-NOWN-see-**AY**-shi̱n. Watch out for this mispro*nun*-ciation; it is very common and easy to slip into without hearing yourself do so. It may help to remember that there is no *pronoun* in *pronunciation*.

psalm SAHM. Do not say SAHLM.

The L is silent. See **calm**.

pulpit PUUL-pit, not PUHL-pit.

The pul- in *pulpit* should sound like the verb to *pull*. The pronunciation PUHL-pit, in which pul- rhymes with *dull*, was not listed in dictionaries before the 1960s, and is not preferred by any of my current sources.

---

a = at • a̱ = woman • ah = spa • ahr = car • air = fair • ay = hay • aw = saw • ch = chip • e = let • e̱ = item • ee = see • eer = deer • i = sit • i̱ = direct • ng = sing • o̱ = connect • oh = go • oo = soon • or = for • oor = poor • ow = cow • oy = toy • sh = she • th = thin • th = them • u̱ = focus • uh = up • ur = turn • uu = pull, took • y, eye = by, pie • zh = measure

Q

qualm KWAHM. Do not say KWAHLM. The L is silent. See **calm**.

quasi KWAY-zy or KWAY-sy.

The A should be long, as in *quake*; the I should be long, as in *sigh*; and the S may be either soft, as in *rose*, or hard, as in *case*. Older sources generally prefer KWAY-sy, with the hard S; most current ones prefer KWAY-zy, with a soft S. (Both follow the rule for the English pronunciation of Latin outlined under **data**.) The popular variants KWAH-zee (which is relatively recent) and KWAH-see (the classical Latin pronunciation) are standard but not preferred.

N.B.: The quasi - in *Quasimodo* (the ecclesiastical term for the first Sunday after Easter as well as the name of Victor Hugo's famous hunchbacked character) is an exception. Because *Quasimodo* is formed from the first words of the Latin Introit, *quasi modo geniti infantes* ("As newborn babes . . ." 1 Pet. 2:2), it is pronounced like the classical Latin: KWAH-see-**MOH**-doh (or often, KWAH-zee-**MOH**-doh).

quay KEE.

KEE is preferred by all current sources. KAY (which rhymes with *pay*) and KWAY (which rhymes with *sway*) sometimes appear as alternatives, the former considerably more often than the latter.

Worcester (1884) shows that by the late nineteenth century the consensus was already strongly in favor of KEE: Of ten authorities polled by him, only one preferred KAY, and KWAY is not listed.

querulous KWER-uh-l<u>u</u>s, not KWEER-uh-l<u>u</u>s.

In *querulous*, peevish, complaining, and *query*, a question, inquiry, the E of quer- is pronounced differently. In *querulous* the E is short, as in *quench*, *quell*, and *Quentin*. In *query* the E is long, as in *queen* and *queasy*.

Today *querulous* is so often mispronounced KWEER-uh-l<u>u</u>s (KWEER- as in *queer*) that one dictionary (*Webster's Ninth*) now includes the variant. Be careful to avoid this vogue pronunciation. Also, do not say KWAHR-uh-l<u>u</u>s or KWOR-uh-l<u>u</u>s (like *quarrel* + *us*); this mispronunciation is an eccentric resurrection of the obsolete word *quarrelous*, which was once used to mean either quarrelsome or querulous. The alternative pronunciation KWER-yuh-l<u>u</u>s, in which a Y sound precedes the U in the second syllable, appears in most current sources, but KWER-uh-l<u>u</u>s is universally preferred. See **query**.

query KWEER-ee.

Query is now increasingly mispronounced KWER-ee, or sometimes KWAIR-ee. KWER-ee (with a short E, as in *quest*), now appears as an alternative in *Webster's Ninth*; *Webster's New World Guide* calls it "occasional." KWAIR-ee (KWAIR- rhyming with *pair*) does not to my knowledge appear in any dictionary. Both are vogue pronunciations (see Appendix). The proper pronunciation is KWEER-ee (like *queer* + -*y*). See **querulous**.

quietus kwy-EE-t<u>u</u>s.

Because the word *quiet* is so prominent in *quietus*, many speakers mistakenly pronounce it like *quiet*, with the accent on the first syllable: KWY-<u>it</u>-<u>u</u>s. This mispronunciation has persisted since the early part of this century, but has yet to find its way into a dictionary.

Quietus is divided qui·e·tus, the I and E are long (as in *sigh* and *see*) and the accent falls on the E: kwy-EE-t<u>u</u>s. You can hear the pronunciation in the iambic rhythm of these lines from the famous soliloquy in Shakespeare's *Hamlet*:

> For who would bear the whips and scorns of time . . .
> When he might his *quietus* make,
> With a bare bodkin?

R

rabid RAB-id. Do not say RAY-bid.

Rabid and *rabies* have different pronunciations. *Rabid* has a short A, as in *rabbit*. *Rabies* has a long A, as in *ray*.

The beastly mispronunciation RAY-bid, with the long A of *ray*, is quite recent, appearing in only two of my current sources, *Webster's Ninth* (1985) and *Webster's New World* (1984). The latter notes that it occurs most when the word is used to mean "affected with rabies."

Be careful: Don't let RAY-bid bite you, or you will surely start foaming at the mouth and uttering all sorts of other monstrosities.

ratiocination RASH-ee-AHS-i-**NAY**-shin.

Ratiocination is reasoning, the process of exact or logical thinking. The primary stress falls on the penultimate—next to last—syllable, with lighter accents on the first and third syllables: RASH-ee-AHS-i-**NAY**-shin.

ration RASH-in or RAY-shin.

---

a = at • a̲ = woman • ah = spa • ahr = car • air = fair • ay = hay • aw = saw • ch = chip • e = let • e̲ = item • ee = see • eer = deer • i = sit • i̲ = direct • ng = sing • o̲ = connect • oh = go • oo = soon • or = for • oor = poor • ow = cow • oy = toy • sh = she • th = thin • t̲h̲ = them • u̲ = focus • uh = up • ur = turn • uu = pull, took • y, eye = by, pie • zh = measure

---

Both pronunciations are standard and have been heard in cultivated speech for at least a hundred years. By the 1930s RASH-in was the prevailing pronunciation in England. American dictionaries preferred RAY-shin until the 1940s, but since then RASH-in has been listed first.

In his authoritative *Desk-Book of Twenty-five Thousand Words Frequently Mispronounced* (1929), Frank H. Vizetelly writes that RASH-in is the pronunciation "common to the armies of Great Britain and the United States, and Dr. Craigie [an editor of the *OED*] suggests that this may be due to the adoption of the word, in the sense of provisions, from the French."

realtor REE-ul-tur. Do not say REE-luh-tur.

A great many educated speakers have difficulty with this word. I have heard it mispronounced by announcers on radio and television, by professionals and people in high places, and by REE-ul-turs themselves. The problem comes from inadvertently switching the L and the A, which results in the nonstandard pronunciation REE-luh-tur. It can be resolved by carefully saying the word *real* and following it with *-tur*. See **athlete**, **February**, **jewelry**, **nuclear**.

recognize REK-ug-nyz.

Be sure to pronounce the G. Do not say REK-uh-nyz.

refuge REF-yooj. Do not say REF-yoozh.

The second syllable rhymes with *huge*. See **refugee**.

refugee ref-yoo-JEE or REF-yoo-jee.

This word is now frequently mispronounced ref-yoo-ZHEE or REF-yoo-zhee, with a ZH sound (like S in *vision*) replacing the traditional soft G of the last syllable. [Soft G is pronounced like J; you can hear it in *gauge* (GAYJ), *assuage* (uh-SWAYJ), *agitate* (AJ-i-tayt), and the exclamation *gee* (JEE).] The ZH sound occurs in the second G of *garage* (guh-RAZH) and *negligee* (neg-li-ZHAY), but dictionaries do not recognize the pronunciation ref-yoo-ZHEE for *refugee*. Like the second G in *negligent* (NEG-li-jent), the G in *refugee* has the sound of J: ref-yoo-JEE.

Refugee may be accented on the first or last syllable, depending on the stress of your sentence: "We visited the REF-yoo-jee center"; "Thousands of ref-yoo-JEEZ were crossing the border each day." See **refuge**, **siege**.

regime ray-ZHEEM or ri-ZHEEM or ruh-ZHEEM.

All three pronunciations are standard, but the first is most often preferred. Be careful not to say ri-JEEM.

remonstrate ruh-MAHN-strayt, not REM-uhn-strayt.

The accent is on the second syllable, like *demonstrative* (de-MAHN-struh-tiv).

reparable REP-ur-uh-buul, not ruh-PAIR-uh-buul. See **comparable**, **irreparable**.

repartee rep-ur-TEE or rep-ahr-TEE, not rep-ur-TAY or rep-ahr-TAY.

The word *repartee*, a quick, witty reply, or conversation filled with clever replies, came into English in the mid-seventeenth century from the French *repartie*, a retort. At first it was often spelled like the French, or sometimes with a final Y, *reparty*, but the modern spelling, which had appeared by 1712, predominated by 1800.

From the beginning the English pronunciation has been rep-ur-TEE, which retains the French accent on the final syllable (-tee) with its French long E (EE) sound. This was the only pronunciation recognized by dictionaries until the 1960s, when rep-ur-TAY (-TAY as in *take*) leapt into currency. Rep-ur-TAY is wrong because it is pseudo-French: It is based on false analogy with the current English pronunciations of such French words as *negligee* (neg-li-ZHAY) and *divorcée* (di-vor-SAY)—and possibly even *touché*, which is so often used to acknowledge a trenchant remark—not on the original French source of *repartee*, in which the final syllable is pronounced like *tea*.

Though rep-ur-TAY is now very commonly heard in educated speech, ten out of eleven current sources polled prefer rep-ur-TEE, and three of these do not recognize rep-ur-TAY. See **envelope**, **lingerie** (for more on pseudo-French pronunciations).

respite RES-pit. Do not say ruh-SPYT.

The accent should be on the first syllable, and the second syllable should be pronounced like *pit*. The mispronunciation ruh-SPYT, which misplaces the accent and changes the short I to a long I, rarely appears in dictionaries and is not preferred by any current source. It dates back, however, to at least 1900, probably earlier, and so deserves membership in the infamous Antiquarian Beastly Mispronunciation Society, whose disreputable members include AWF-ten for *often*, HYT-TH or HYTH for *height*, and mis-CHEE-vus or mis-CHEE-vee-us for *mischievous*. See **height**, **mischievous**, **often**.

ruse ROOZ. Do not say ROOS.

Ruse, a trick, deception, came into the language from French in the early seventeenth century, and for over three hundred years was pronounced ROOZ, to rhyme with *muse* and *fuse*. Then all of a sudden, in 1961, ROOS (rhymes with *goose*) made a startling debut in *Webster* 3 as the *preferred* pronunciation. 'Twas a clever ROOZ that ROOS pulled, but it did not fool everyone. I checked sixteen sources printed since *Webster* 3: four prefer ROOS,* but eleven of the other twelve do not even recognize it. Say ROOZ.

*Two of these are Merriam-Webster dictionaries based on *Webster* 3; the other two are Houghton Mifflin dictionaries.

S

sacrilegious SAK-ri-**LIJ**-us or SAK-ri-**LEE**-jus.

SAK-ri-**LIJ**-us was once an infamous beastly mispronunciation, but it has long been used by educated speakers and now unquestionably prevails in cultivated speech.

Need I say more? Yes—a word of explanation to those of you who might still take exception to SAK-ri-**LIJ**-us, and some consolation for those who have been unjustly criticized for saying it this way.

In 1929, the eminent American linguist and lexicographer Frank H. Vizetelly, in his *Desk-Book of Twenty-five Thousand Words Frequently Mispronounced*, gives the pronunciation SAK-ri-**LEE**-jus, but notes that "the word is now more frequently heard [SAK-ri-**LIJ**-us]." In 1934, *Webster* 2 sanctioned SAK-ri-**LIJ**-us as an alternative, and in 1936, John G. Gilmartin, in *Everyday Errors in Pronunciation*, underscored this for those unable to buy or consult that great wordbook: "Until 1934," he writes, "the third syl-

---

a = at • a̲ = woman • ah = spa • ahr = car • air = fair • ay = hay • aw = saw • ch = chip • e = let • e̲ = item • ee = see • eer = deer • i = sit • i̲ = direct • ng = sing • o̲ = connect • oh = go • oo = soon • or = for • oor = poor • ow = cow • oy = toy • sh = she • th = thin • th̲ = them • u̲ = focus • uh = up • ur = turn • uu = pull, took • y, eye = by, pie • zh = measure

lable... had to rhyme with *tea*. Now the third syllable may also be... pronounced *lij* to rhyme with *bridge*."

By the 1940s, SAK-ri-**LIJ**-us was so prevalent that the *American College Encyclopedic Dictionary* and Kenyon and Knott put it first, the latter remarking that for British and American speakers alike, SAK-ri-**LIJ**-us "is probably due to the analogy of [*sacrilege*, pronounced SAK-ri-lij] and the unrelated [*religious*]." Finally, eight out of twelve sources printed since 1960 prefer SAK-ri-**LIJ**-us, and *Webster's New World Guide* (1984) observes that "the earlier standard [SAK-ri-**LEE**-jus] is much less frequently heard."

That, I hope, will settle the issue. Let there be no more bad blood between the orthodox pronouncers who say SAK-ri-**LEE**-jus and the recusant pronouncers who say SAK-ri-**LIJ**-us. Dogma has changed, and the offense has now become law. However, a final word of caution to both parties: Do be careful to *spell* the word properly. Even eagle-eyed copy editors sometimes overlook the misspelling *sacreligious*. See **schism**.

sandwich SAND-wich. Do not say SAN-wich.

This word should be pronounced exactly as it is spelled. Do not drop the D and say SAN-wich, even in rapid speech, for this seemingly innocuous mispronunciation is construed by many as a sign of a careless speaker.

sanguine SANG-gwin (-gwin rhymes with *win*).

This is the only recognized pronunciation. Do not say SANG-gwyn (-gwyn rhyming with *wine*) or SANG-gween (-gween rhyming with *queen*).

schedule SKEJ-ool or SKEJ-uul.

In British and, to a lesser extent, Canadian English speech, SHED-yool and SHEJ-ool are the prevailing pronunciations. To the American ear these sound unnatural and stilted, and are best avoided by American speakers.

schism Properly, SIZ-um. Now often SKIZ-um.

Most words beginning with sch- are pronounced either SK-, as in *school* and *scheme*, or (generally only in words and names of German, Yiddish, or Hebrew origin) SH-, as in *schwa*, *schnauzer*, *Schmidt*, and *schmaltz*. *Schism*, however, is a special exception.

The word came into English in the late fourteenth century from the Greek and Latin *schisma*, through the Old French *cisme* or *scisme*, to the Middle English *scisme*. Of the numerous spellings that arose in the next two hundred years, *scisme* was the most common, and it was not until the seventeenth century that the H began to reassert itself from the original Latin and Greek. (In 1644, Milton used *scism*; twenty-four years later Izaak Walton spelled it *schism*.)

The burgeoning crop of English dictionaries in the eighteenth century served to establish *schism* as the standard spelling, but the pronunciation SIZ-um, based on earlier spellings without the H, had already been the norm for centuries. Thus English gained yet another incongruity between a word's form and its sound—but that, my friend, is what gives the language its character (and, unfortunately, what makes it so difficult to pronounce).

Dictionaries continued to cherish this little discrepancy, this *schism* between spelling and pronunciation; however, around the beginning of this century the spelling pronunciation SKIZ-um began to catch on among speakers unfamiliar with the word's history, who made the natural but erroneous association with other English words beginning with sch-. (There may also have been some attempt on the part of certain scholars to promote SKIZ-um on analogy with the pronunciation of the original Latin and Greek; if so, it would represent one of the only times a pronunciation mandated by pedants was taken up by hoi polloi.) Upon its arrival, SKIZ-um was denounced by various authorities (W. H. P. Phyfe, for example), and until the 1960s dictionaries continued to give only SIZ-um.

SKIZ-um made its lexicographic debut in *Webster* 3 (1961), but it was hardly an auspicious one, for the editors marked it "unacceptable to many." I grew up in the 1960s, and until a few years ago I had no idea that SIZ-um existed in a dictionary; I had always heard and said SKIZ-um, so I never thought to look it up and make sure it was correct. If you now say SKIZ-um, I imagine you will be as shocked as I was to discover that SIZ-um is the preferred pronunciation in *every* dictionary and pronunciation guide I have consulted, which includes at least ten printed since 1980—several of which do not even recognize SKIZ-um.

As a SKIZ-um sayer, there are two ways you can respond to this information: You can rise up in fury and vilify the entire profession of lexicography by claiming that it's run by a bunch of ivory-tower eggheads with too much wax in their ears, or you can sit back for a moment and consider why the weight of authority is still so unswervingly behind SIZ-um—pondering the singular history of the word; how hoary and intransigent the established pronunciation seems in comparison to the rash and juvenile SKIZ-um, which arose out of ignorance; and the fact that the clergy, who perhaps are most knowledgeable about *schisms*, are generally conscientious about pronouncing (and denouncing) them properly. I don't think you'll have to think about it too long before you come around, and —take my word for it—after you've said it a few times, SIZ-um won't seem odd to your ear at all (especially when you know you have every dictionary ever printed to back you up).

N.B.: A very recent *schism* in the pronunciation of *schism* has yielded the variant SHIZ-um, which appears in *Webster's Ninth* (1985) labeled "appreciably less common." SKIZ-um is understandable as a misapplication of the SK sound for sch- in words from Greek and Latin. SHIZ-um, on the other hand, is a fanciful pronunciation for which there is no legitimate, or even illegitimate, authority.

schizophrenia SKIT-suh-**FREE**-nee-uh, not SKIT-suh-**FREN**-ee-uh.

Schizophrenia is divided schiz·o·phre·ni·a. Because the third syllable (-phre-) is accented and ends in a vowel, the vowel (E) is long: SKIT-suh-**FREE**-nee-uh. The pronunciation SKIT-suh-**FREN**-ee-uh is based on false analogy with *schizophrenic* (SKIT-suh-**FREN**-ik). To justify the short E sound of **FREN** for the third syllable, the word would have to be divided schiz·o·phren·i·a.

The mispronunciation SKIT-suh-**FREN**-ee-uh first appeared in *Webster* 3 (1961), preceded by the word *sometimes*, meaning it was infrequently heard. Of the thirteen sources printed from 1962 to 1987 that I polled, all prefer SKIT-suh-**FREE**-nee-uh, and only two recognize SKIT-suh-**FREN**-ee-uh. Before 1960, the preferred pronunciation was SKIZ-uh-**FREE**-nee-uh, with the Z pronounced like Z in *zebra* instead of like TS in *skits*. This older pronunciation is still listed as an alternative in some dictionaries today; however, it has been almost entirely supplanted by SKIT-suh-**FREE**-nee-uh. See **hysteria**, **wisteria**.

secreted si-KREE-tid, not SEE-kri-tid.

Secreted is the past tense and past participle of the verb to *secrete* (si-KREET), which may mean to discharge through the process of secretion, or to hide, conceal, as, "They decided to *secrete* the incriminating documents in the wall safe." (Nowadays they usually just shred them.) When *secrete* means to discharge through secretion, no one mispronounces it. When it means to hide, however, there has

---

a = at • a̱ = woman • ah = spa • ahr = car • air = fair • ay = hay • aw = saw • ch = chip • e = let • e̱ = item • ee = see • eer = deer • i = sit • i̱ = direct • ng = sing • o̱ = connect • oh = go • oo = soon • or = for • oor = poor • ow = cow • oy = toy • sh = she • th = thin • t̲h̲ = them • u̱ = focus • uh = up • ur = turn • uu = pull, took • y, eye = by, pie • zh = measure

been a tendency of late to shift the accent to the first syllable, especially in the form *secreted*.

There once was a verb to *secret*, spelled without an E at the end; it became obsolete by the middle of the eighteenth century, and since then *secrete*, with an E at the end, has been the standard spelling. Had the verb *secret* survived, perhaps today the pronunciation SEE-krit and SEE-kri-tid would be sanctioned. It did not, however, and current dictionaries universally prefer si-KREET and si-KREE-tid.

N.B.: The adjective *secretive* is now pronounced SEE-kri-tiv, with the accent on the first syllable, when it means disposed to keep secrets. However, when it means pertaining to secretion, it is pronounced si-KREE-tiv.

senile SEE-nyl. Do not say SEN-yl.

Senile is accented on the first syllable, which rhymes with *glee*; the second syllable should rhyme with *file*.

Formerly the word was sometimes pronounced SEE-nil, with the second syllable rhyming with *pill*. This variant has gradually faded from the dictionaries and in the last thirty years a new one has risen in its place: SEN-yl (SEN- as in *send*, -yl like *aisle*). I am not sure whether this pronunciation is of British or American origin, though I suspect the former. It is not preferred by any of my current sources, and I imagine it eventually will go the way of the earlier unsuccessful pretender to the throne of SEE-nyl, which, despite its venerable age, shows no signs of infirmity or dotage. See **textile**.

servile SUR-vil or SUR-vyl. (The first is preferable.)

SUR-vil (-vil as in *evil*) is the traditional American pronunciation preferred by most current sources. SUR-vyl (-vyl rhymes with *file*) is originally British. See **textile**.

short-lived SHORT-LYVD, not SHORT-LIVD.

The I is long, as in *alive*, not short, as in *give*. See **long-lived** (for an explanation of why the long I is preferred in the adjectival combining form *-lived*).

siege SEEJ. Do not say SEEZH.

SEEZH, with the ZH sound of *seizure*, is a very recent mispronunciation, perhaps no more than ten years old. I first heard it four or five years ago from some of the announcers on National Public Radio's news programs, and I have heard it used since by television newscasters.

I am not sure if the media started the mispronunciation, but they certainly were instrumental in promoting it to vogue pronunciation status (see the Appendix for a discussion of this term). SEEZH now appears in *Webster's Ninth* (1985), preceded by the word *also*, which means it is "appreciably less common." Let's keep it that way. *Siege* and *besiege* came into English in the thirteenth-century, and for at least as long as dictionaries have recorded pronunciation (about two hundred and fifty years) these words have been pronounced SEEJ and bee-SEEJ. This is the marking of all current sources, which, except for *Webster's Ninth*, do not recognize the erroneous SEEZH. See **liege**, **refuge**, **refugee**.

similar SIM-i-lur. SIM-yoo-lur is nonstandard.

Be careful not to insert a YOO sound in the second syllable of this word and say SIM-yoo-lur, as though the word were spelled *simular*. This is a first-class beastly mispronunciation. See **irrelevant**, **jewelry**, **nuclear**.

sinecure SYN-i-kyoor, not SIN-i-kyoor.

Sinecure, from the Latin *sine cura*, without a care, entered English in the 1660s. Since then it has been used either specifically to mean a salaried ecclesiastical position that does not involve caring for souls, or generally to mean any paid position with little or no responsibility.

The pronunciation SIN-i-kyoor (SIN- like *sin*) has been listed by dictionaries for a little over fifty years, but the traditional pronunciation, SYN-i-kyoor (SYN- like *sign*), is preferred by nearly all sources, past and present.

sonorous Properly, suh-NOR-u̱s. Now often SAHN-ur-u̱s.

SAHN-ur-u̱s, with the accent on the first syllable, is British. The traditional American pronunciation is suh-NOR-u̱s, with the accent on the second syllable. It is still preferred by most current American dictionaries, including *Random House II* (1987), *Webster's Ninth* (1985), *Everyday Reader's* (1985), and *Webster's New World* (1984). See **inculcate**, **infiltrate**, **obfuscate**, **paradigm**, **precedence**.

species SPEE-sheez, not SPEE-seez.

The origin of the spurious SPEE-seez begins not in the slime of billions of years past, but just a paleontologic wink of an eye ago in *Webster 3* (1961), where it appeared labeled "appreciably less frequent." (Whether it was endogenous [born in America] or exogenous [imported from Great Britain, Australia, or outer space] is not certain.) SPEE-seez proved to be a very hardy little beast, for by the 1970s it had invaded several other dictionaries, and by 1980 it had reached maturity as a major vogue pronunciation. (See the Appendix for a discussion of this term.)

Yes, what was once but a lowly "*SPEE-seez infrequentus*" has in just the last few years become the formidable "*SPEE-seez reiteratus.*" It seems that every other speaker these days—whether biologist, member of the bar, bartender, or bezonian*—is saying SPEE-seez. Yet, despite its astounding popularity, no current dictionary prefers it.

*A beggar or scoundrel (pronounced bi-ZOH-nee-a̱n).

This, indeed, makes my heart glad, for to me, SPEE-seez is painfully overrefined. No one would be caught dead saying PRES-ee-us for *precious* or SPES-ee-al for *special*, lest he or she be accused of being SOH-see-uh-lee (socially) am-BIS-ee-us (ambitious) and intellectually SOO-pur-**FIS**-ee-al (superficial). Q.E.D.: SPEE-seez is specious (SPEE-shus), and should go the way of all faddish pronunciations—into extinction.

spherical SFER-i-kal, not SFEER-i-kal.

The first syllable of *spherical* (spher-) should not be pronounced SFEER, with a long E sound, like *sphere* or the first syllable of *spheroid* (SFEER-oyd). *Sphere* is monosyllabic, which makes the E long; *spheroid* is divided sphe·roid, and because the E ends the accented syllable, it is long. The first syllable of *spherical*, however, ends after the R, spher·i·cal, and so the E is short, as in *fetch* or *ferry*: SFER-i-kal. See **atmospheric**, **hysteria**, **schizophrenia**.

spontaneity SPAHN-ta-**NEE**-i-tee, not SPAHN-ta-**NAY**-i-tee.

Pronounce the third, accented syllable with a long E, like the word *knee*, not with a long A, like the word *nay*. See **deity**, **homogeneity**.

status Properly, STAY-tus, not STAT-us. See **data**.

strength STRENGKTH, not STRENTH or STRAYNTH.

The consonant blend NG (as in *sing*) should be audible in *strength* (STRENGKTH). See **length**.

---

a = at • a = woman • ah = spa • ahr = car • air = fair • ay = hay • aw = saw • ch = chip • e = let • e = item • ee = see • eer = deer • i = sit • i = direct • ng = sing • o = connect • oh = go • oo = soon • or = for • oor = poor • ow = cow • oy = toy • sh = she • th = thin • th = them • u = focus • uh = up • ur = turn • uu = pull, took • y, eye = by, pie • zh = measure

succint suk-SINKT, not suh-SINKT.

This word is increasingly mispronounced. Pronounce the first C in *succint* like a K, and the second like an S: suk-SINKT. See **accessory**, **flaccid**.

summarily Traditionally, SUHM-ur-uh-lee. Now, suh-MAIR-uh-lee.

This is a eulogy upon an obsolescent pronunciation. In the last several decades there has been a marked tendency for speakers to shift the stress in certain words from the first syllable to the second, apparently for greater emphasis. For example, *exquisite, despicable, hospitable, lamentable*, and *explicable*, which for years most speakers pronounced with the accent on the first syllable, are now improperly accented by many on the second syllable.

Most current dictionaries still prefer the stress on the first syllable for the five examples mentioned above. For *summarily*, however, the tide unfortunately has turned. Until the 1960s, *summarily* was also accented on the first syllable, like many adverbs formed from three-syllable adjectives having their accent on the first syllable: *similar, similarly; succulent, succulently; sumptuous, sumptuously; seminal, seminally*; and *summary*, SUHM-ur-uh-lee. In the last thirty years, however, as more and more speakers adopted the "emphatic" pronunciation—with the accent on the second syllable—dictionaries have abandoned SUHM-ur-uh-lee in favor of suh-MAIR-uh-lee, which is now sometimes the only pronunciation given. See **despicable**, **explicable**, **exquisite**, **hospitable**, **lamentable**.

superfluous soo-PUR-floo-<u>us</u>.

Do not say soo-pur-FLOO-<u>us</u> or soo-PUR-fuh-l<u>us</u>.

I have heard a number of well-educated and even some prominent speakers mispronounce this word soo-pur-

FLOO-us, shifting the accent from the second syllable
(-per-) to the third (-flu-). This is not recognized by dictionaries. I have never heard the mispronunciation soo-
PUR-fuh-lus, but I include it because it appears in one
source—*Webster* 3 (1961)—marked "unacceptable to
many."

Both soo-pur-FLOO-us and soo-PUR-fuh-lus are nonstandard. Soo-pur-FLOO-us is wrong because it misplaces
the accent; soo-PUR-fuh-lus is a mispronunciation caused
by metathesis, the transposition of letters, sounds, or syllables in a word. With *superfluous*, be careful to stress
the *per* and follow it with *flu*: soo-PUR-floo-us. See **superfluity**.

superfluity SOO-pur-**FLOO**-i-tee.

This is the only recognized pronunciation. Unlike the adjective *superfluous*, which is accented on the second syllable (-per-), the noun *superfluity*, overabundance, excess,
is accented on the third syllable (-flu-). See **superfluous**.

supposed suh-POHZD, not suh-POH-zid.

In all of its applications, *supposed* should be pronounced
in two syllables, not three. When *supposed* is used as the
past tense or past participle of *suppose*, it is less often
mispronounced: "We suh-POHZD they were there"; "It
has been suh-POHZD." Mispronunciation occurs chiefly
when the word is used as an adjective: "Much was said
about their suh-POHZD [often suh-POH-zid] infractions of
the law." In this adjectival sense, the word means imag-
ined, believed, received as true. We do not say imagin-
ed, believ-*ed*, or receiv-*ed*, so why say suppos-*ed*?

Supposed is so frequently mispronounced that most
current dictionaries now include the three-syllable variant, but all prefer the two-syllable pronunciation: suh-
POHZD. The adverb is pronounced suh-POH-zid-lee. See
alleged.

T

tercel TUR-s<u>e</u>l.

A *tercel* is a male hawk, especially a peregrine falcon. The name of the Toyota automobile, pronounced tur-SEL, comes from this bird. I am not necessarily suggesting that we change the pronunciation of the car, only that we retain the proper pronunciation for the bird. See **prelude**.

textile TEK-st<u>i</u>l or TEK-styl.

American speakers pronounce most words ending in -ile with an obscure or "silent" I, as in *evil*, *pupil*, and *fossil*. Conversely, in Great Britain, the prevailing tendency is to pronounce words ending in -ile with a long I, as in *file*. Thus, for *hostile*, *futile*, and *fertile*, Americans say HAHS-t<u>i</u>l, FYOO-t<u>i</u>l, FUR-t<u>i</u>l, and the British say HAHS-tyl, FYOO-tyl, FUR-tyl. This distinction holds true for *fragile*, *docile* (British DOH-syl), *versatile*, *imbecile*, *agile*, *sterile*, *virile*, *missile*, *projectile*, *volatile*, *tactile*, *ductile*, *puerile*, and the adjective *mobile* (the city in Alabama and the moving sculpture are pronounced MOH-beel). *Reptile*, **servile**, and **juvenile** are also traditionally pronounced REP-t<u>i</u>l, SUR-v<u>i</u>l, JOO-v<u>e</u>-n<u>i</u>l by Americans, but in the last twenty or thirty years the long I has been increasingly heard, and today usage is probably about evenly divided, though most current American dictionaries give the "silent" I pronunciation first.

These, then, are the general tendencies, to which of course there are several exceptions, the foremost being *gentile*, pronounced with a long I on both sides of the Atlantic (probably so as not to be confused with the word *gentle*); *senile* and *infantile*, which Americans have pronounced with a long I for at least sixty years; and *mercantile*, for which a third variant, MUR-k̠an-teel, sprang up about thirty years ago and is now probably heard as often as MUR-k̠an-tyl or MUR-k̠an-til.*

As for *textile*, it too seems to be joining the list of exceptions. Most current sources prefer TEK-styl, with the British long I, and TEK-stil, with the American "silent" I, though still listed in good standing, is less often heard.

theater THEE-uh-tur.

Properly, this word has three syllables, but when pronounced quickly in the flow of conversation, it often comes out THEER-tur. That is hardly objectionable, however, when compared with the truly beastly mispronunciation thee-AYT-ur, which *Webster's Ninth* (1985) says occurs most often in southern speech, but which *Random House II* (1987) calls "characteristic chiefly of uneducated speech" and *Webster's New World Guide* (1984) affirms is "generally disapproved."

---

*Webster 2 (1934) notes that the words *camomile*, *crocodile*, *exile*, and *reconcile* are exceptions because they do not actually contain the suffix *-ile*.

---

a = at • a̠ = woman • ah = spa • ahr = car • air = fair • ay = hay • aw = saw • ch = chip • e = let • e̠ = item • ee = see • eer = deer • i = sit • i̠ = direct • ng = sing • o̠ = connect • oh = go • oo = soon • or = for • oor = poor • ow = cow • oy = toy • sh = she • th = thin • t̠h = them • u̠ = focus • uh = up • ur = turn • uu = pull, took • y, eye = by, pie • zh = measure

tortuous TOR-choo-<u>us</u>.

Tortuous, when used properly, is rarely mispronounced. However, a different word, *torturous*, is often mistakenly used in its place, and when this confusion in usage occurs, the concomitant error is mispronunciation.

Torturous means involving torture, extremely painful. It has *two* Rs, and is pronounced TOR-chur-<u>us</u>, like *torture* plus *us*. *Tortuous* means crooked—either literally, in the sense of twisting, winding, circuitous, or figuratively, in the sense of tricky, devious. It has *one* R, and is pronounced TOR-choo-<u>us</u>, like *torch* plus OO and *us*. If you are careful to distinguish these two words in usage, you should have no trouble with their pronunciation.

tousled TOW-zuuld.

TOW- rhymes with *how*; -zuuld rhymes with *pulled*. Make sure the S sounds like a Z. Do not say TOW-suuld or TUH-suuld.

transfer (verb) trans-FUR; (noun) TRANS-fur.

Everyone accents the noun *transfer* on the first syllable, which is correct, but many speakers today also accent the verb to *transfer* on the first syllable when it is properly the *second* that should receive the stress.

When a two-syllable word serves as both a noun and a verb, it is the general rule (or, if that word reminds you of schoolmarms wielding rulers—custom) that the noun is accented on the first syllable and the verb on the second. Thus *transfer*, *transport*, and *transplant* are accented on the first syllable when used as nouns (a TRANS-fur, a TRANS-port, a TRANS-plant), but when used as verbs they should be accented on the second syllable (to trans-FUR, to trans-PORT, to trans-PLANT).

Furthermore, most of the two-syllable verbs beginning with the prefix *trans-* that do not also function as nouns are likewise properly accented on the second syllable. This is generally observed with the words *transpire*, *transgress*, and *transmute*, but with *transpose*, *transact*, *transcend*, *transmit*, *transcribe*, and especially *translate*, many speakers today misplace the accent, putting it on the first syllable when it should be on the second.

transient Properly, TRAN-shent.

TRAN-shent is the traditional American pronunciation—the only one given by older American dictionaries and the one still preferred by current American authorities. All other variations listed in American dictionaries today are apparently British in origin, for they first appeared in the *OED* and other British dictionaries of the first half of this century.

In the last decade or so, broadcasters have used such an astonishing number of variants for *transient* (chief among them, TRAN-zee-ent) that the public has become utterly confused and misled. This is unfortunate, because the lexicographic evidence is clear and the verdict is unanimous: TRAN-shent is the preferred pronunciation. Is it really necessary to say it any other way?

trauma Traditionally, TRAW-muh. Now usually TROW-muh.

TROW-muh (TROW- rhyming with *cow*), has been listed for about forty years; since the 1960s it has been preferred by most authorities. Earlier dictionaries recognized only TRAW-muh (TRAW- rhyming with *law*). See **glaucoma**.

traverse Properly, TRAV-urs, not truh-VURS.

"This represents one of the few cases—exceptions to the general rule," writes John G. Gilmartin in *Everyday Errors in Pronunciation* (1936), "in which a verb of two syllables must be accented on the first syllable."

Usage has changed, and current dictionaries no longer reflect Gilmartin's preference. This, however, is one endangered species I am compelled to champion. When everywhere speakers are busy creating exceptions to the rule that bisyllabic verbs are accented on the second syllable, someone must stick his neck out for the established exception that suddenly everyone is making conform to the rule.

In his famous dictionary of 1755, which set the standard for the language in both England and America for over a hundred years,* Samuel Johnson gives TRAV-urs for both verb and noun, noting that the word "was anciently accented upon the last syllable." What queer atavism is this, that truh-VURS should reemerge after more than two hundred years? From Johnson's day until the 1960s, TRAV-urs was the proper pronunciation, and, though down on its luck in the past quarter-century, TRAV-urs is still used by many cultivated speakers. (*Everyday Reader's Dictionary* [1985] gives only TRAV-urs.) If truh-VURS can be resurrected, then surely TRAV-urs—the *modern* English pronunciation—can recover from its wounds and fight again. See **decrease**, **transfer**.

tumult TYOO-mult or TOO-mult.

Tumult is one of the words I used to mispronounce habitually. All through high school and college I said TUHM-ult (TUHM- as in *tumble*), because TUH was the sound I

---

*Sidney I. Landau writes that "Johnson fashioned a work that engendered such respect that for well over a century it was without peer as the most authoritative dictionary in English. Revised by Henry John Todd in 1818 and again in 1827, Todd-Johnson, as it came to be known, was esteemed the best of dictionaries in both England and America until well into the nineteenth century. Indeed, it was Webster's ambition, to which he devoted the better part of his life, to supplant Todd-Johnson's place in America as the standard work." (From *Dictionaries: The Art and Craft of Lexicography* [New York: Charles Scribner's Sons, 1984], pg. 56.)

thought I heard in the first syllable of *tumultuous* (which is properly pronounced too-MUHL-choo-<u>us</u> or tuu-MUHL-choo-<u>us</u>, sometimes tyoo- or tyuu-).

Not until I became an editor did I bother to check the pronunciation in a dictionary, where to my surprise I found that the U in the first syllable should be pronounced like the U in *tumor* (TYOO-mur or TOO-mur). I don't care much for surprises like this, so now I make it a habit to confirm my pronunciation of even the most familiar words. It's a good practice if you like to be right.

turgid TUR-jid.

The G in *turgid* is soft, which means it has the sound of J, as in *rage* or *gypsy*. Do not say TUR-gid with a hard G, as in *bargain* or *gaggle*.

---

a = at • <u>a</u> = woman • ah = spa • ahr = car • air = fair • ay = hay • aw = saw • ch = chip • e = let • <u>e</u> = item • ee = see • eer = deer • i = sit • <u>i</u> = direct • ng = sing • <u>o</u> = connect • oh = go • oo = soon • or = for • oor = poor • ow = cow • oy = toy • sh = she • th = thin • <u>th</u> = them • <u>u</u> = focus • uh = up • ur = turn • uu = pull, took • y, eye = by, pie • zh = measure

U

ultimatum uhl-ti-MAY-tum, not uhl-ti-MAH-tum.

Ultimatum entered the language about 1730. It comes directly from Latin, and for well over a hundred years has been anglicized according to the rule for the so-called English pronunciation of Latin outlined under **data**, which states that vowels ending accented syllables have their long English sounds.

Until the 1960s, dictionaries recognized only the pronunciation uhl-ti-MAY-tum, in which the A in the third, accented syllable is long, as in *mate*. Since then the pronunciation uhl-ti-MAH-tum (MAH- as in *Mata Hari*) has appeared in most dictionaries, but is not preferred. It is a de-anglicized pronunciation—showing a regression from English to the classical Latin—which should be scrupulously avoided. See **data** (for the English pronunciation of Latin) and **cadre**, **junta**, **lingerie** (for more on de-anglicization).

undertaking uhn-dur-TAY-king.

When the word *undertaking* is used to mean an enterprise or endeavor, it should be accented on the third syllable: uhn-dur-TAY-king. When pronounced UHN-dur-tay-king, with the accent on the first syllable, the word refers to the profession of the mortician.

usurp Traditionally, yoo-ZURP. Now usually yoo-SURP.

Properly, the S has the sound of Z: yoo-ZURP. This is the only pronunciation listed in the *Century* (1914) and *Webster* 2 (1934), and the preference of Kenyon and Knott (1949) and the *American College* (1953). By the 1960s, however, yoo-SURP had *usurped* the throne of yoo-ZURP, and today it reigns in all but two current sources—*Funk & Wagnalls Standard* (1980) and *Webster's New Twentieth Century* (1983).

usury YOO-zhu-ree, not YOO-zuh-ree or YOO-suh-ree.

The S in *usury* has the ZH sound of the S in *vision* and *measure*.

V

vagaries Traditionally, vuh-GAIR-eez or vuh-GER-eez (E in GER- as in *get*). Now usually VAY-guh-reez.

Vagaries is the plural of *vagary*—a wild fancy, eccentric action, or unpredictable event—which entered the language in the late sixteenth century, formed apparently from the Latin verb *vagari* (wuh-GAH-ree), to wander. Like the Latin, *vagary* and *vagaries* were accented on the second syllable (-ga-), as in these seventeenth-century lines from Milton: "They changed their minds / Flew off, and into strange *vagaries* fell / As they would dance."

Throughout the nineteenth century, dictionaries gave only the pronunciation vuh-GAY-ree, with a long A in the second syllable, following the rule for the English pronunciation of words taken from Latin, in which vowels ending accented syllables have their long English sounds (see **data** for the full citation of this rule). Eventually, as speakers began to blend the long A of *gay* into the adjacent R, *vagary* came to be pronounced vuh-GAIR-ee, or sometimes vuh-GER-ee (E in GER- as in *get*), and this change was reflected in the preferred pronunciations of major dictionaries of the first half of this century, including the *OED* (completed in 1928), *Webster* 2 (1934), and the landmark *American College* (1947).

Between about 1900 and 1930, the pronunciation VAY-guh-ree, with the accent on the first syllable, began to gain currency in educated British speech. It appeared as an alternative in the 1924 edition of Daniel Jones's *English Pronouncing Dictionary* (in which the author claims to represent the colloquial pronunciation of those who have been "educated at the great public boarding schools"), and subsequently in the *Shorter Oxford English Dictionary*, edited, among others, by H. W. Fowler and C. T. Onions, and published in 1933.

Then it was but a short Atlantic cruise from England's upper crust to America's Anglomaniacs, who snapped up this latest Etonian gewgaw and, through the infamous trickle-down effect, bestowed it on the masses. VAY-guh-ree did not appear in American dictionaries until the 1960s, but by then it had become so prevalent in American speech that *Webster* 3, which introduced it in 1961, gave it precedence, and the influential *American Heritage* followed suit in 1969.

Authorities since have split into warring factions. The latest college edition of the *American Heritage* (1982) and Merriam-Webster's most recent abridgment of *Webster* 3, *Webster's Ninth* (1985), continue to prefer VAY-guh-ree, and they have been joined by the *NBC Handbook* (1984). Hanging tough for vuh-GAIR-ee are *Scribner–Bantam* (1979); *Oxford American* (1980); *Funk & Wagnalls Standard* (1980); *Webster's New World* (1984); *Everyday Reader's* (1985); and *Random House II* (1987).

Daniel Boorstin, the distinguished American historian and Librarian of Congress, says vuh-GAIR-eez. William Safire, the renowned language columnist for *The New York*

---

a = at • a̲ = woman • ah = spa • ahr = car • air = fair • ay = hay • aw = saw • ch = chip • e = let • e̲ = item • ee = see • eer = deer • i = sit • i̲ = direct • ng = sing • o̲ = connect • oh = go • oo = soon • or = for • oor = poor • ow = cow • oy = toy • sh = she • th = thin • t̲h̲ = them • u̲ = focus • uh = up • ur = turn • uu = pull, took • y, eye = by, pie • zh = measure

Times, claims that most people say VAY-guh-reez, and in an article on the subject he adjured the dictionaries to "get with it." Whether you prefer to be with it or, like me, are ever skeptical of the imported pronunciation and defer to tradition over trend—this will determine which way the dictionaries ultimately go, for there are no vuh-GAIR-eez (or VAY-guh-reez) in the profession of lexicography. However you choose to say it, though, try not to say VAG-uh-ree (VAG- as in *vagabond*), which is an out-and-out beastly mispronunciation.

valet VAL-it. Now often va-LAY or VAL-ay.

In America, where most gentlemen prefer to dress themselves and do their own errands, there is little use for this word. It survives, however, as the term for an anthropomorphic rack for holding clothing and other personal effects, and in the odd custom of "valet parking," which seems to have been created to provide a socially acceptable outlet for the potentially destructive impulses of young male drivers. For "valet parking," the pronunciation VAL-ay is now so entrenched that it would be pedantic and pointless to try to change it. The rack, on the other hand, since it is designed to substitute for the servant, should have the traditional pronunciation: VAL-it. (If the thing could talk, I'm sure it would respectfully request that you say VAL-it.)

Should you have need of this word in any other context, you might appreciate knowing that Kenyon and Knott, in their *Pronouncing Dictionary of American English* (1949), call the pronunciations va-LAY and VAL-ay "pseudo-French," and *Webster* 2 (1934) notes that the word has been anglicized since the seventeenth century. Thus, like *claret* and *jacket* (also old bisyllabic borrowings from French that end in -ET), *valet* is properly pronounced with the accent on the first syllable and the final T sounded: VAL-it. This is the preference of all older authorities and eight out of ten current ones. See **envelope** (for more on pseudo-French pronunciations).

vase VAYS or VAYZ. Do not say VAHZ or VAWZ.

VAYS (rhymes with *base* and *case*) is the prevailing and preferred American pronunciation, though VAYZ (rhymes with *phrase* and *phase*) is used by many cultivated speakers. Both have been listed in American dictionaries for well over a hundred years. The pronunciations VAHZ (rhymes with *Oz*) and VAWZ (rhymes with *cause*) are British.

vaudeville VAWD-vil or VOHD-vil. Also VAW-duh-vil.

VOHD-vil was the only pronunciation given by nineteenth-century American dictionaries, and was the preferred pronunciation of American authorities in the first half of this century. In the last thirty years, however, VAWD-vil has prevailed, and most current authorities now prefer it. Also acceptable is the three-syllable variant VAWD-uh-vil; it appeared as an alternative in *Webster* 2 (1934) and the *American College* (1947), and is listed first by Kenyon and Knott (1949), but in the last twenty years it has been heard less frequently. Another three-syllable variant, VOHD-uh-vil, is "especially British," according to *Webster* 2.

vegetable VEJ-tuh-buul, not VEJ-e-ta-buul.

One day you may encounter a member of the so-called Language Police who will badger you about your grammer, scoff at your colloquialisms, pluck the prepositions from the ends of your perfectly natural sentences to stick them somewhere infinitely more awkward, and insist that the proper pronunciation of *vegetable* is VEJ-e-ta-buul, with four painfully distinct syllables. I include this entry for your protection should this ever happen to you.

In the 1940s, Kenyon and Knott and the *American College Encyclopedic Dictionary* gave precedence to VEJ-tuh-buul, and since then the three-syllable pronunciation has thoroughly dominated the four-syllable one, which is now rarely heard in educated speech—or, for that matter, in any class of speech other than that used by the Language Police. Four syllables are appropriate when reading old poetry aloud, such as this seventeenth-century couplet from Andrew Marvell's "To His Coy Mistress": "My *vej-e-ta-ble* love should grow / Vaster than empires, and more slow." In nearly all other situations, however, the pedantic VEJ-e-ta-buul sticks out like an armoire in a studio apartment. Though most of my current sources still dutifully record it, only one (*Funk & Wagnalls Standard*) prefers it. "To everything there is a season," sayeth the prophet, "a time to plant, and a time to pluck up that which is planted." The four-syllable variety of *vegetable* is now an archaism, and in colloquial speech it is virtually extinct.

vehicle VEE-i-kuhl. Do not sound the H.

venereal vuh-NEER-ee-al. Do not say vuh-NAIR-ee-al.

Television journalist and talk show host Geraldo Rivera says vuh-NAIR-ee-al, and, as we all know, when someone with a microphone mispronounces something, it can quickly lead to an epidemic of imitation. The Pronunciation-General's Warning is here affixed for your protection: vuh-NAIR-ee-al is not recognized by dictionaries. The safe way to say it is vuh-NEER-ee-al.

vendor VEN-dur, not VEN-dor or (in legalese) ven-DOR.

Lawyers and judges habitually overpronounce certain common words, perhaps because they were taught to do so, but more likely because it keeps the layperson in awe of the solemnity and grandiloquence of the legal profession. Whatever the case, I move that VEN-dorz and ven-DORZ, along with dee-FEN-dants and JOOR-orz—which the average citizen calls VEN-durz, di-FEN-di̱nts, and JOOR-urz—constitute a menace to society, and therefore should stay in the courtroom and not be released on their own recognizance, until such time as they can be tried, pronounced guilty, and sentenced to life imprisonment. See **juror**, **mentor**, **predator**.

vertebrae   VUR-tuh-bree, not VUR-tuh-bray.

Vertebra, the singular, and *vertebrae*, the Latinate plural (the anglicized *vertebras* is also standard), are both often mispronounced VUR-tuh-bray. The error apparently goes back pretty far, and, like all old errors, this one has its distinguished proponents. In *The American Language* (1937 edition), H. L. Mencken claims that for *vertebrae*, the pronunciation *"vertebray* is commoner than *vertebree,"* and cites its appearance seven years earlier as a variant in Larsen and Walker's *Pronunciation: A Practical Guide to American Standards*.

Despite the august advocacy of Mencken, VUR-tuh-bray did not get into a dictionary until 1961, when *Webster* 3 labeled it "unacceptable to many." Though this official disparagement has since been dropped, out of seven current sources polled only two prefer VUR-tuh-bray for the plural *vertebrae*, four do not recognize the pronunciation, and only one gives it as an alternative for the singular *vertebra*, for which it is a particularly beastly mispronunciation. See **algae**.

---

a = at • a̱ = woman • ah = spa • ahr = car • air = fair • ay = hay • aw = saw • ch = chip • e = let • e̱ = item • ee = see • eer = deer • i = sit • i̱ = direct • ng = sing • o̱ = connect • oh = go • oo = soon • or = for • oor = poor • ow = cow • oy = toy • sh = she • th = thin • t̲h̲ = them • u̱ = focus • uh = up • ur = turn • uu = pull, took • y, eye = by, pie • zh = measure

vice versa VY-see VUR-suh or VY-suh VUR-suh. Do not say VYS VUR-suh.

This is not the same *vice* as in "vice squad" or "Miami Vice." That *vice*, which rhymes with *ice* and *nice*, comes from the Latin *vitium*, a fault, defect, and means depravity, immoral behavior. The *vice* in *vice versa* is the ablative of the Latin *vicis*, change, turn, alternation, and is used in English as a preposition meaning in place of, instead of, and is pronounced in two syllables: VY-see.

The proper pronunciation of *vice versa*, therefore, is VY-see VUR-suh, with both vowels in *vice* long (rhyming with *high* and *sea*). When the phrase is said quickly, though, the second syllable of *vice* is often obscured to VY-suh or VY-si. This pronunciation has been heard in educated speech for over forty years, and is now generally preferred. The one-syllable VYS, which first appeared in *Webster* 3 (1961)—listed last—is common but not recommended for its injustice to the origin and history of the word.

Out of ten current sources polled, six prefer VY-suh or VY-si VUR-suh, three prefer VY-see VUR-suh, and only one prefers VYS VUR-suh, though because it is so frequently heard it appears in six others. If you've been accustomed to saying the vicious VYS, and if the venerable VY-see sounds a bit too precious to your ear, then go with the versatile VY-suh and no one will notice the difference.

victuals VIT-ulz.

You can take your cue on this word from Jed Clampitt and the other Beverly Hillbillies: VIT-ulz is the only standard pronunciation. (More often than you might think, the plain folk of the world are correct in their pronunciation of plain English words, for sometimes the result of a little education is a lot of overrefinement.)

Victuals dates back to 1300. The C is left over from the Latin root, *victualis*, pertaining to food; it was dropped in the Middle English *vitaille*, provisions, and reinstated in the sixteenth and seventeenth centuries. The spelling pronunciation (see Appendix) VIK-choo-<u>u</u>lz, which is sometimes heard in educated speech, is nonstandard and not countenanced by dictionaries. Pronounce *victuals* to rhyme with *whittles*.

visa VEE-zuh, not VEE-suh.

Lately, more and more people have begun to pronounce this word VEE-suh, with an S rather than a Z sound, perhaps because of the influence of the voice-overs in the television commercials for the popular credit card, where it is habitually mispronounced. In 1961, *Webster 3* recognized the variant, but only one source printed since— *Webster's Ninth*, also a Merriam-Webster dictionary—acknowledges VEE-suh, marking it "appreciably less common."

Visa came into English from French around 1830. In French, a single S between vowels is soft—that is, pronounced like English Z in *maze* or S in *rose*—and this has been the standard English pronunciation of the S in *visa* since the word entered the language. The pronunciation VEE-suh, with a hard S sound, as in *vista* or *viscous*, is appropriate in Spanish, but not in English. Say VEE-zuh.

W

wash WAHSH or WAWSH. Do not say WAHRSH or WAWRSH.

Certain speakers allow the sound of R to insinuate itself between the A and S of *wash*, pronouncing the word as if it were spelled *warsh*. Only two sources record the pronunciations WAHRSH and WAWRSH, which contain the R sound: *Webster's Ninth* (1985) calls them "chiefly Midland," and *Webster 3* (1961) calls them "chiefly substandard."

In the cautious lingo of linguists, what this chiefly means is that the R-colored pronunciations of *wash* are either in circumscribed use by an indeterminate portion of the population in the middle United States and do not reflect "the general practice of the nation" (Noah Webster's influential standard of propriety), or they are in more geographically widespread though still less frequent use than WAHSH and WAWSH, but are disapproved of or considered uncultivated by many.

Simply put, pronouncing the word *wash* with a R sound between the A and the S should be avoided in careful speech.

wastrel WAY-str<u>e</u>l. Do not say WAH-str<u>e</u>l (WAH- as in *wasp*).

Wastrel has the long A (AY) of its source, the verb to *waste* (WAYST).

In 1961, *Webster* 3 included the pronunciation WAH-str<u>e</u>l, preceded by the word *sometimes* to indicate that it was infrequent. Since then the increasing (though still occasional) use of WAH-str<u>e</u>l among educated speakers has led *Webster's Ninth* (1985)—the most current abridgment of *Webster* 3—to list it as an alternative, this time preceded by the italicized word *also*, meaning that it is no longer infrequent but "appreciably less common" than WAY-str<u>e</u>l. (See Sometimes and Also in the Appendix.)

WAH-str<u>e</u>l does not appear in *Webster* 2 (1934)—the predecessor of *Webster* 3—nor, for that matter, in any of my other sources. Merriam-Webster's recognition of WAH-str<u>e</u>l may be commendable descriptive lexicography, but in light of the rest of the dictionary-making community's unanimous disregard of this erroneous pronunciation one can only conclude that, had it not been planted by the vigilant and sedulous linguists of *Webster* 3 and nurtured by the faithful editors of *Webster's Ninth*, it probably would have gone the way of all waste into the trash can of language. Instead we must wait for the arrival of the next unabridged Merriam-Webster dictionary to see if WAH-str<u>e</u>l will make yet another unprecedented leap into currency beside WAY-str<u>e</u>l, which the weight of authority confirms is the only standard pronunciation.

werewolf WEER-wuulf (WEER- as in *weary*).

There are three recognized pronunciations for this word: WEER-wuulf; WUR-wuulf (WUR- rhyming with *fur*); and

---

a = at • <u>a</u> = woman • ah = spa • ahr = car • air = fair • ay = hay •
aw = saw • ch = chip • e = let • <u>e</u> = item • ee = see • eer = deer
• i = sit • <u>i</u> = direct • ng = sing • <u>o</u> = connect • oh = go • oo =
soon • or = for • oor = poor • ow = cow • oy = toy • sh = she •
th = thin • <u>th</u> = them • <u>u</u> = focus • uh = up • ur = turn • uu =
pull, took • y, eye = by, pie • zh = measure

WAIR-wuulf (WAIR- rhyming with *bear*). This is the order in which they appear in most current dictionaries. To remember it, and so recall the preferred pronunciation, ask yourself this question: "We were where?" (*We* as in WEER-wuulf, *were* as in WUR-wuulf, and *where*—unaspirated H—as in WAIR-wuulf.)

The pronunciation WAIR-wuulf first appeared in *Webster* 3 in 1961. Of the twelve sources printed since then that I polled, two do not list it, eight put it third, one gives it second (*Webster's Ninth*), and only one current dictionary—*Random House II*—prefers it. The pronunciation WEER-wuulf is preferred by the other eleven sources.

wisteria wi-STEER-ee-uh. Also, for the spelling *wistaria*, wi-STAIR-ee-uh.

Wisteria, the climbing shrub that blooms in lovely pendent clusters of flowers, is often associated in literature and in American popular culture with the porticoes and verandas of stately eighteenth- and nineteenth-century dwellings, particularly the antebellum mansions of the American South. It was named in honor of Caspar Wistar, an American anatomist (1761–1818), and is sometimes spelled *wistaria*, with the A of Wistar in place of the E. *Webster* 2 (1934) prefers *Wistaria*, with a capital W, calling it the correct form for the genus and the only spelling approved by the International Code of Botanical Nomenclature. This opinion, however, is not reflected in most other dictionaries, past and present, which prefer *wisteria* and give *wistaria* an alternative in good standing.*

---

*Language columnist Michael Gartner explains that the confusion is the fault of a Harvard botanist, Thomas Nuttall (1786–1859). In naming the genus after Wistar, Nuttall apparently intended to spell it *wistaria* but accidentally wrote *wisteria* instead. It was published this way, and ever since the error has been the norm. ("Words," *Newsday*, November 1, 1987.)

This creates a quandary for the pronouncer of this word. Is the pronunciation wi-STEER-ee-uh correct when the word is spelled *wistaria*? Some current dictionaries say it is. Is the pronunciation wi-STAIR-ee-uh permissible for the more common spelling *wisteria*? A few current sources allow it. Does this mean that when dictionaries differ we can say it however we want to? Well, yes and no.

Consistency is always the best solution to this sort of problem. Usage has long shown a preference for the spelling *wisteria,* with an E, and the pronunciation wi-STEER-ee-uh, and I wholeheartedly recommend spelling and pronouncing the word this way. However, if you come across the spelling *wistaria,* with an A, which is far less frequent in current writing, then out of respect for the word's history say wi-STAIR-ee-uh. Just don't say wi-STAIR-ee-uh when the word is spelled *wisteria*. See **hysteria, schizophrenia.**

wizened WIZ-end (WIZ- as in *wizard*).

Wizened means withered, shrunken, shriveled. This participial adjective was created in the early 1500s from one of the oldest words in English, the verb to *wizen* (WIZ-en), to dry up, wither, which dates back to the ninth century. In the late eighteenth century, *wizen* also became an adjective and for the next hundred years was used interchangeably with *wizened*. To further confuse things, in the nineteenth century the words were often spelled *weazen* and *weazened* (the *OED* cites examples of these forms from Washington Irving, Charles Dickens, William Makepeace Thackeray, and W. S. Gilbert). From these variant spellings (which, according to *Webster* 2, are now obsolete or dialectal) we inherit the pronunciations WEE-zen and WEE-zend, which some current dictionaries still give as alternatives for the universally preferred pronunciations, WIZ-en and WIZ-end.

The pronunciation WY-zind (WY- as in *wise*), which is

not recognized by dictionaries, is sometimes heard today from educated speakers who have learned the word from reading and arrived at their pronunciation on no other authority but their own conjecture.

wont WAWNT (rhymes with *gaunt*); or WUHNT (rhymes with *hunt*); or WOHNT (like *won't*). Occasionally, WAHNT (like *want*).

Wont may mean accustomed, and is used attributively, as: "That night he retired at the hour he was *wont* to"; or it may mean custom, usual practice, as: "While visiting Europe, she ran five miles each morning, as was her *wont* at home."

This word dates back to the twelfth century, and for most of its history was far more common in speech than it has been in the present century. In the 1940s, Kenyon and Knott, in their *Pronouncing Dictionary of American English,* noted that "to many *wont* is not vernacular, and hence is subject to spelling pronunciation, and perhaps to the influence of *won't*."

When a word starts to fade from conversational use and is encountered mainly in print, its traditional pronunciation gradually becomes unfamiliar and people start to guess how it should be pronounced. In the last hundred years, as *wont* fell out of our everyday vocabulary, new pronunciations for it proliferated.

Between 1900 and 1934, along with WUHNT, the traditional American pronunciation, American dictionaries began to record WOHNT, which they marked as especially British. (Conversely, the *OED*—the British paragon of English lexicography, completed in 1928—gives WOHNT followed by WUHNT, described as "now chiefly U.S.") Over the next thirty years, two more pronunciations came into being: WAWNT and WAHNT. Both appear in Kenyon and Knott, who label them "less frequent," but by the year

1961 WAWNT had overtaken all the others and was listed first in *Webster 3*.

Since then WAWNT has been preferred by most American dictionaries, which usually list the British WOHNT next, with WUHNT, the earlier preferred pronunciation, slipping to third place. WUHNT now shares the back of the pack with the final variant recorded by Kenyon and Knott, WAHNT, which fell behind at the outset and is marked by dictionaries today as having very limited currency.

---

a = at • a̲ = woman • ah = spa • ahr = car • air = fair • ay = hay •
aw = saw • ch = chip • e = let • e̲ = item • ee = see • eer = deer
• i = sit • i̲ = direct • ng = sing • o̲ = connect • oh = go • oo =
soon • or = for • oor = poor • ow = cow • oy = toy • sh = she •
th = thin • t̲h̲ = them • u̲ = focus • uh = up • ur = turn • uu =
pull, took • y, eye = by, pie • zh = measure

X

Xanthippe zan-TIP-ee or zan-THIP-ee.

Xanthippe was the wife of Socrates, and she is as proverbial for henpecking and browbeating the old gadfly as he is revered for dismembering his disciples with casuistry and syllogisms. Since the late seventeenth century we have been using *Xanthippe,* spelled with a capital X, to mean an ill-tempered, shrewish woman—a termagant (TUR-muh-gant), virago (vi-RAY-goh or vi-RAH-goh).

Dictionaries countenance both zan-TIP-ee and zan-THIP-ee when the word is spelled with an H, but for the alternative spelling *Xantippe,* without the H, only the pronunciation zan-TIP-ee is correct.

Xavier ZAY-vee-ur, ZaY-vyur; or ZAV-ee-ur, ZAV-yur.

The Spanish pronunciation is hah-VYAIR.

Xavier should be pronounced in either three or two syllables, and the X should be pronounced like Z in *Zanzibar.* Beastly mispronunciation occurs when speakers attempt to pronounce the X like *ex-* in *example* or *excuse,* which winds up adding a fourth syllable to the word. Do not say ig-ZAY-vee-ur or ek-SAY-vee-ur; these pronunciations are nonstandard.

xenophobia ZEN-uh-**FOH**-bee-uh, not ZEE-nuh-**FOH**-bee-uh.

Xenophobia, fear and hatred of foreigners, or of anything strange or foreign, first appeared in print shortly after 1900. Its antonym, *xenomania* (ZEN-uh-**MAY**-nee-uh), an inordinate attachment to foreign things, was coined thirty years earlier but is rarely used today.

There is a fable for our times that explains how the mispronunciation ZEE-nuh-**FOH**-bee-uh (ZEE- as in *zebra*) came to exist side by side with the proper ZEN-uh-**FOH**-bee-uh. In the small number of words in which it occurs, the combining form *xeno-* was always pronounced ZEN-oh (with the short E of *Zen*), except in the gaseous element *Xenon* (ZEE-nahn), symbol Xe. Until very recently there was no confusion about this; dictionaries quietly gave their ZEN- pronunciations and people quite contentedly used them.

Then one day, as the story goes, someone unfamiliar with the conventions of the language—probably a foreign spy—methodically and malevolently started to mispronounce all the ZEN- words, saying ZEE- instead. Soon all the *xenomaniacs*—in particular those members of the literati who are continually searching for new outlets for their *xenophilia* (ZEN-uh-**FIL**-ee-uh), love of foreigners and foreign cultures—began to copy this evil example, and the beastly mispronunciation ZEE-nuh-**FOH**-bee-uh stampeded its way into the dictionaries. Today ZEE-nuh-**FOH**-bee-uh is recognized by three sources, and those who use it, pedants and plebeians alike, apparently neither know nor care that ZEN-uh-**FOH**-bee-uh was once the true and only native pronunciation.

Would you like a moral? Buy liberty bonds, wave the flag at every opportunity, and, above all, say ZEN-uh-**FOH**-bee-uh. See **paradigm.**

Y

yarmulke YAHR-m<u>u</u>l-kuh. Also, YAH-m<u>u</u>l-kuh.

Nine out of eleven current sources agree that this Yiddish word for skullcap should be pronounced as it is spelled: YAHR-m<u>u</u>l-kuh, with the R and L clearly articulated. Of the two dissenters, one (*American Heritage,* New College), prefers YAH-m<u>u</u>l-kuh, with the R dropped but the L pronounced, and the other *(Webster's Ninth)* prefers YAH-m<u>u</u>h-kuh, with both the R and L dropped.

In New York City, where I grew up, I remember hearing YAH-muh-kuh almost exclusively; consequently, I thought for a long time that the word was spelled *yamaka.* Despite its popularity there and in other sections of the country, the pronunciation YAH-muh-kuh is uncultivated because it grossly misstates the name of a ritual object with a long linguistic as well as sacred tradition. (This probably accounts for why YAH-muh-kuh appears in only one other dictionary besides *Webster's Ninth.*) The pronunciation YAH-m<u>u</u>l-kuh, on the other hand, is an acceptable alternative (listed by five current sources), for it accommodates speakers who normally drop their Rs in such words as *farther, cart, park,* but retains the sound of the L.

ye (article, meaning "the") <u>THUH</u> or <u>THEE</u>.

Ye, meaning "the," is very often confused in pronunciation with *ye,* the archaic form of *you,* which is pronounced

YEE. This is because most people are unaware that the Y in the *ye* that means "the" is not a real Y—it is the modern representation of the Anglo-Saxon TH character þ, which looks like Y. Thus, *ye*, meaning "the," should be pronounced just like *the*: THUH before a word beginning with a consonant, THEE before a word beginning with a vowel. YEE, I'm afraid, is just a beastly old spelling pronunciation (see Appendix for a discussion of this term).*

So, dear reader, when next *ye* go to *Ye* Olde Laundromat or *Ye* Olde Taco Shoppe, or lodge at *Ye* Compleat Motor Inne, *ye* can say *ye* word right and show thy friends how infinitely clever thou art.

yolk YOHK. Do not say YOHLK.

Yolk rhymes with *poke*. The L is silent.

your YUUR (UU like double OO in *look*), often variable to YOOR (rhymes with *boor*) or YOR (rhymes with *for*).

This word is very often pronounced YUR (rhymes with *fur*). There is nothing inherently wrong with YUR; it appears in all current dictionaries as the prevailing pronun-

---

*Why bother to spell it with a Y, you ask, when the Y doesn't stand for a Y and isn't pronounced like a Y? Respect for tradition, I suppose. To retain the quaint flavor of an archaic word. Besides, if we simplified things by changing the Y in *ye* to TH, the word—and the delightful confusion in its pronunciation—would no longer exist. That would be regrettable, for there's nothing like a little arcanum to liven up one's day.

---

a = at • a̱ = woman • ah = spa • ahr = car • air = fair • ay = hay • aw = saw • ch = chip • e = let • e̱ = item • ee = see • eer = deer • i = sit • i̱ = direct • ng = sing • o̱ = connect • oh = go • oo = soon • or = for • oor = poor • ow = cow • oy = toy • sh = she • th = thin • t̲h̲ = them • u̱ = focus • uh = up • ur = turn • uu = pull, took • y, eye = by, pie • zh = measure

ciation when the word is unstressed in a sentence, as, "Is that your hat?" (as opposed to the stressed, "Is this your hat or his?"). However, in more formal situations where you wish or need to speak carefully—such as delivering a speech, appearing in a television or radio interview, or making yourself clear over the telephone—it is as inappropriate as *gonna* for *going to, wanna* for *want to, lemme* for *let me,* and *nuthin* (or worse, *nut'n*) for *nothing.*

Z

zoology zoh-AHL-uh-jee, not zoo-AHL-uh-jee.

The first syllable (zo-) rhymes with *go,* not with *do.*

The mispronunciation zoo-AHL-uh-jee (with the first syllable pronounced like the word *zoo*) has existed since at least the beginning of this century, and has been heard from many otherwise cultivated speakers—Katharine Hepburn, for example, in the 1939 film *Bringing Up Baby.* Despite its prevalence among the educated, dictionaries have stubbornly refused to recognize it. It appears in *Webster 3* (1961) preceded by the symbol ÷, meaning that many found it unacceptable, and current authorities confirm this judgment. *Webster's New World Guide* (1984) remarks that it is not considered standard, and even the most recent unabridged American dictionary, *Random House II* (1987), gives only zoh-AHL-uh-jee. *Webster's Ninth* (1985) is the one source that has capitulated and sanctioned the mispronunciation, though not without some trepidation: The editors have cleverly disguised it as zuh-WAHL-uh-jee, in which the ambiguous zuh- could be construed as being an underarticulated zoh-.

Zoology formerly was printed with a dieresis (dy-ER-uh-sis)—two small dots—above the second O, to show that it is pronounced as a separate syllable. Likewise, until about thirty years ago *cooperate* and *preeminent* were usually printed with a dieresis, or often a hyphen, to indicate that the double Os and double Es are pronounced distinctly. Now all three words appear without these pronunciation aids, and though no one would dream of saying koo-AHP-ur-ayt or PREE-muh-n_e_nt, millions blithely say zoo-AHL-uh-jee. This pronunciation is ridiculous, for it requires three Os (*zoo-ology*) and makes the word sound as if it means the study of zoos. (ZOO-luh-jee has more basis in reason, but apparently no one had the sense to mispronounce it that way.) Perhaps we should return to printing the word with a dieresis, or better, a hyphen between the Os. I will support any measure, however draconian, that will help speakers separate the *zo-* from its *-ology.*

zoological zoh-uh-LAHJ-i-k_a_l, not zoo-uh-LAHJ-i-k_a_l. See **zoology**.

zoologist zoh-AHL-uh-jist, not zoo-AHL-uh-jist. See **zoology**.

zounds ZOWNDZ.

Zounds, which came into the language about 1600, is an archaic exclamation of wonder or anger, "a euphemistic abbreviation," says the *OED,* for *by God's wounds.* The word appears occasionally in the plays of Shakespeare and other English dramatists of the seventeenth and eighteenth centuries, and in productions of such works I have often heard the actors mispronounce it ZOONDZ or ZWOONDZ.

I suspect that this is the result of an assumption on the part of certain speech and dialect coaches, or directors, that because the oath incorporates the word *wounds* it should be pronounced with the OO sound of *wounds* and not the OW sound (as in *out*) of diphthong OU.

This assumption is false. John Walker's *Critical Pronouncing Dictionary* of 1791 shows clearly that up until his time *wound* was pronounced WOWND (to rhyme with

bound and *found*), and the pronunciation WOOND
(rhyming with *marooned*) had only recently come into
vogue in "polite society." By 1836, WOOND was so established that the English orthoepist Benjamin Humphrey
Smart called WOWND "the old-fashioned pronunciation."

Zounds, therefore, being an old-fashioned word, follows the old-fashioned pronunciation: ZOWNDZ. This is
the marking of all my sources but one—*Webster's Ninth*
(1985)—which lists ZOWNDZ or ZWOWNDZ followed by
the mispronunciations now popular on the stage: ZOONDZ
and ZWOONDZ. For alternative spellings incorporating
W, such as *'dswounds,* I suppose that the pronunciation
ZWOWNDZ is acceptable, but *zounds,* people!—there is
no authority for the pronunciations ZOONDZ and
ZWOONDZ. A historical nicety is at stake here, which
actors, in particular, should take care to preserve. The
word should *not* be pronounced with an OO sound to
conform with the modern pronunciation of *wound*; it
must have the OW sound of the old-fashioned pronunciation.

---

a = at • a̱ = woman • ah = spa • ahr = car • air = fair • ay = hay •
aw = saw • ch = chip • e = let • e̱ = item • ee = see • eer = deer
• i = sit • i̱ = direct • ng = sing • o̱ = connect • oh = go • oo =
soon • or = for • oor = poor • ow = cow • oy = toy • sh = she •
th = thin • tẖ = them • u̱ = focus • uh = up • ur = turn • uu =
pull, took • y, eye = by, pie • zh = measure

Appendix

Except where otherwise indicated, cross-references in this Appendix refer to other entries in the Appendix.

Also

Used in most dictionaries to indicate a pronunciation that is less common, usually much less so, than the preceding pronunciation(s), as, *Visa*: VEE-zuh, also VEE-suh. In most cases pronunciations marked "also" or "sometimes" are best avoided, for they are very often spelling pronunciations, vogue pronunciations, or substandard pronunciations that the editors have decided to be lenient about, which may not appear at all in other dictionaries. See Sometimes, Spelling Pronunciation, Substandard, Vogue Pronunciation.

Alternative Pronunciation or Alternative

An alternative pronunciation is any pronunciation not listed first in a dictionary. Alternative pronunciations may or may not be as common as the first pronunciation listed; however, in most cases—especially when there is more than one—they are either less common or less desirable than the pronunciation listed first.

"Alternative" and "alternative pronunciation" are generally used interchangeably in the text with "variant pronunciation" and "variant," although the latter terms sometimes have a more disparaging connotation, which can be apprehended from context. See Preferred Pronunciation, Standard, Variant Pronunciation.

Anglicize, Anglicization

To anglicize is to make English, conform to English modes and usages. *Anglicization* refers either to something that has been made English or to the natural and inevitable process by which a foreign word or phrase be-

173

comes English in its form, usage, and pronunciation. *Anglicize* and *anglicization* come from the Latin *Anglicus,* pertaining to England or to the Angles, a northern Germanic people who, along with the Saxons and the Jutes, invaded and settled England in the fifth century A.D.

Today, through the influence of mass media, words adopted from foreign languages are often anglicized in a decade or even less; until recently, however, anglicization in pronunciation usually took anywhere from fifty to well over a hundred years, depending on how common the word was in everyday speech. **Foyer,** for example, came into English from French in the 1850s, and in cultivated speech was pronounced fwah-YAY, like the French, for at least seventy-five years. By 1934, the word was in common use, and *Webster* 2 recorded two anglicized pronunciations after the original French fwah-YAY: FOY-ay (which is half-anglicized), and FOY-ur (which is fully anglicized). Today fwah-YAY is passé, FOY-ay is passing gradually out of use, and FOY-ur, the completely anglicized pronunciation, is most commonly heard. See **cadre, foyer, junta, largess, lingerie** in the Guide.

Colloquial

Conversational, used in conversation, of everyday speech. A colloquial pronunciation is not necessarily incorrect or substandard. Some colloquialisms are entirely appropriate in cultivated speech. Each case, therefore, must be considered individually. See Cultivated Speech, Substandard.

Cultivated Speech, Speakers

One meaning of the verb to *cultivate* is to devote special attention to with the aim of improving. In this book, the adjective *cultivated* means refined by study and training, marked by skill and taste. A synonym might be *cultured,* although that word may have objectionable overtones for many. Cultivated pronunciation occurs at all levels of society, in every region, just as uncultivated speech is heard from rich and poor, educated and uneducated alike in all parts of the country.

In short, cultivated speakers are those who have arrived at their pronunciation not simply by imitation but also by practice. Cultivated speech is the way in which such conscientious speakers choose to agree how words should be pronounced—and especially, how that is represented in the dictionaries.

Cultivated speech very often allows for some variation, and its preferences may or may not reflect "the general practice of the nation" (Noah Webster's phrase). Dictionaries have always recorded what is cultivated, even if it is no longer generally practiced; and even as they sanction more and more of what is uncultivated—what older dictionaries might have called erroneous

—they continue to preserve and uphold a standard for cultivation in the very process of redefining it.

Current

Used of dictionaries to mean in general circulation since 1980. On some occasions I have used this term to include certain sources that were printed before 1980 but were widely available after that date, and are still considered authoritative (e.g., *Webster* 3), as well as others that have gone out of print in the 1980s and are no longer available, but are still used by many (e.g., *American Heritage,* New College). See Modern, Recent.

Educated Speakers, Speech

In general, same as Cultivated Speakers, with a diploma or two thrown in. A distinction should be made, however: Educated speakers are not *always* cultivated, for just as knowledge does not guarantee wisdom, so an education does not necessarily result in good pronunciation (except perhaps in British public schools and at Oxford and Cambridge, where you either speak their peculiar lingo—known as Received Standard English—or you eat in the refectory alone and never get invited to the "right" parties). Some of the poorest, or most affected, speakers I have ever heard had doctoral degrees. Their knowledge simply did not extend much beyond their specialty, and it most certainly was deficient in the subject of pronunciation. See Cultivated Speakers.

Established

Settled by usage, fixed by long use, rooted in tradition, accepted by many authorities. I have sometimes used *established* to refer to an older pronunciation that may still be ensconced in the dictionaries, but is not necessarily customary or popular today. See Traditional.

Lexicography

The art and craft of making dictionaries.

Lexicographer

"A harmless drudge," as Samuel Johnson put it, who spends countless, though not always joyless, hours taking the measure of the language of the past and the pulse of the language of the present, and redacting these in the form of a dictionary.

Modern

When used of the English language, the term means since the year 1500. In this book the term is used to mean of the twentieth century—modern times. It is distinguished from *current*, which here refers to that which is in print, in use, or in vogue. See Current, Recent.

Nonstandard

This means one of two things: either that a pronunciation does not appear in dictionaries, and so is improper; or it appears in one or more dictionaries labeled "nonstandard," meaning that it is not characteristic of educated speech. See Educated Speech, Recognized, Standard, Substandard.

Noun-Verb and Noun-Adjective Accent

There is a general rule in English governing the pronunciation of words of two syllables that function as either nouns and verbs or as nouns and adjectives: The nouns are accented on the *first* syllable, the verbs and adjectives are accented on the *second* syllable.

For example, *object* has two syllables, and is both a noun and a verb. Therefore, according to the rule, the noun *object* is accented on the first syllable (AHB-jekt) and the verb upon the second (ob-JEKT). *Content* has two syllables, and serves as both a noun and an adjective. The noun *content* is accented on the first syllable (KAHN-tent), and the adjective upon the second (kun-TENT).

Sounds simple enough, right? Ah, but not so fast. There are always some troublesome words. For instance, how did you stress the word *accented* in the preceding paragraph? On the first or the second syllable? According to the rule, the noun **accent** is stressed on the first syllable (AK-sent) and the verb to **accent** is stressed on the *second*: ak-SENT. *Accented*, therefore, should be pronounced ak-SENT-id. This is the proper pronunciation, though fewer and fewer speakers observe it nowadays.

This rule and some of its exceptions are discussed in more detail under **decrease** and **transfer** in the Guide. For discussions of individual cases, see also **accent, frequent, grimace, increase, permit, traverse** in the Guide.

Or

Used in this book (and in various other pronunciation guides) between two or more pronunciations to indicate that they are equally legitimate, though in most cases the first one listed is recommended. See Preferred Pronunciation.

Orthoepist, Orthoepy

Both come from the Greek *orthos,* right, correct, and *epos,* a word. **Orthoepy** is the art and study of correct pronunciation, and an *orthoepist* is an authority on proper pronunciation.

The funny thing about these words is that the doggone orthoepists can't seem to agree how to pronounce them. Get this: For **orthoepy,** the *Century* (1914) gives **OR**-thoh-EP-ee or or-THOH-e-pee; the *OED* (1928) prefers **OR**-thoh-EE-pee and ahr-THOH-i-pee; *Webster* 2 (1934) sanctions OR-thoh-i-pee or or-THOH-i-pee; and *Webster* 3 (1961) lists OR-thoh-wuh-pee and or-THOH-uh-pee. About the only thing these major league lexica can agree on is that the word is pronounced in four syllables. And that, my friend, is the estimable (that's ES-ti-ma-buul) and exact science of **orthoepy** (select one pronunciation from above).

Preferred Pronunciation

In this book, preferred pronunciation has two meanings: (1) the first or only pronunciation listed in a particular dictionary; or (2) the pronunciation listed first by the majority of dictionaries.

Curiously, preferred pronunciation is a concept denied in the explanatory notes of many dictionaries, which often claim that just the most common pronunciations are listed, with no significance attached to their order. This sounds to me like a lot of equivocal bunkum. If that were the case, wouldn't the exact same pronunciations appear in every dictionary, in roughly the same order? And why bother to use usage labels, such as "nonstandard" or "substandard," if there isn't some concept of preference and propriety at work?

No, it just doesn't wash (or should that be WARSH?). Some pronunciations, I'm afraid, have more merit than others, and by examining and comparing the preferences of numerous authorities, as I have sought to do in writing this book, the best among them can be determined. See Alternative Pronunciation, Nonstandard, Standard, Substandard, Variant Pronunciation.

Recent

Recent usually is used in the text as a synonym of *current,* referring to dictionaries in general circulation since 1980, or to a tendency in pronunciation occurring during the past ten to fifteen years. Occasionally it may refer to a slightly longer period, for instance from the 1960s to the present; this sense can be gained from context. See Current, Modern.

Recognized

A recognized pronunciation is one that appears in one or more dictionaries, though it may or may not be standard. If an entry states that a pronunciation is *not* recognized, you may assume, unless the text specifies otherwise, that it is either substandard or nonstandard. See Nonstandard, Standard, Substandard.

Regional, Regionally

A few pronunciations in this book are preceded by the word *regionally*, which means they are especially prevalent in a particular area of the United States, such as New England, the Midwest, or the South. I have tried to avoid advocating or disparaging regional pronunciations, which are (rightfully) a matter of pride to many speakers, for ultimately they are irrelevant to this book, which is concerned with pronunciations and mispronunciations that occur in all parts of the country.

Wherever possible, I have also tried to acknowledge regional pronunciations that are in widespread use and good standing in the dictionaries, or that are fundamentally the same as the preferred pronunciation but for a slight variation in the sound of a vowel or consonant. For example: If, for the word *berry,* half of America says BER-ee and the other half says BAIR-ee, or for *majority* half says muh-JAHR-i-tee and the other half says muh-JOR-i-tee, I say we are saying essentially the same thing. On the other hand, BEER-ee for *berry* or MAY-jur-uh-tee for *majority* would constitute flagrant and beastly mispronunciation.

Sometimes

Used by dictionaries to indicate a pronunciation that occurs infrequently in educated speech—less often than one preceded by "also"—but enough in the opinion of the editors to warrant recognition. Many pronunciations that appear in current dictionaries with this label are actually mispronunciations that have come into vogue. Thus, many of the pronunciations you may find preceded by this term in your dictionary are criticized in this book. See Also, Nonstandard, Or, Spelling Pronunciation, Substandard, Vogue Pronunciation.

Spelling Pronunciation

A pronunciation based on how a word is spelled, which differs from the traditional, established pronunciation. For example, **plantain** is often mispronounced PLAN-tayn, with -tain pronounced as it is in *stain* or *taint,* when it is traditionally (and correctly) pronounced PLAN-tin, with -tain obscured to -*tin,* as in the analogous words *captain* and *mountain.* Similarly, **colander, schism,** and **brooch,** which are properly pronounced KUHL-an-dur, SIZ-um, and BROHCH, are often mispronounced KAHL-an-dur, SKIZ-um, and BROOCH, all interpretations based on spelling—on how col- and sch- and broo- are usually pronounced in other words. Spelling pronunciations that become widespread are eventually dignified as alternative pronunciations, and some even become preferred.

Spelling pronunciations occur most often when the word is unfamiliar and the pronunciation is either guessed at or mimicked. If a speaker who encounters a new word in reading or in conversation fails to check the pronunciation in a dictionary, then begins to pronounce it in whatever way he or she heard it or imagines it should be said, miscommunication, possibly accompanied by embarrassment, may result. Not long ago I was speaking with a magazine publisher who at one point in the conversation uttered the sounds LIK-um. "Lick 'em?" I thought, perplexed, wondering whether I was being insulted. It was several moments before I realized that the word he was trying to say was *lyceum*—pronounced ly-SEE-um!

Standard

A standard pronunciation is accepted, correct, permissible, A.O.K. (is that standard usage?). Standard pronunciations may also be established or recent, alternative or preferred, frequent or somewhat less frequent. Where it was necessary to pass judgment on the relative merit of two or more standard pronunciations, these were my criteria. See Alternative Pronunciation, Established, Nonstandard, Preferred Pronunciation, Recent, Substandard.

Substandard

In this book *substandard* is synonymous with *beastly.* Dictionaries use the term as an innocuous way of saying, "If you pronounce it this way, you're blowing it." I prefer to be jocular or vicious, and since this is "an opinionated guide for the well-spoken," most of the time I call 'em like I see 'em. If I call a pronunciation "substandard" without a qualifying gibe or some invective, then you may presume that your draconian author was feeling lenient that day, and that the pronunciation is still wrong. See Nonstandard, Standard.

Traditional

A traditional pronunciation is one that has a long history of preference in the dictionaries, but which is usually in some stage of being challenged or supplanted by an alternative pronunciation. See Alternative Pronunciation, Established, Preferred Pronunciation.

Variant Pronunciation or Variant

A variant pronunciation, like an alternative pronunciation, is any pronunciation not listed first in a dictionary. Generally the terms are interchangeable. However, I tend to use *alternative* a bit more dispassionately than *variant*, and where there may be a distinction to be drawn in a given entry, you may think of *alternative* as referring to pronunciations in good standing that perhaps for lack of enough history or currency are not preferred, and *variant* as signifying pronunciations whose usage may be more circumscribed, and whose standing may in some cases be questionable. See Alternative Pronunciation, Preferred Pronunciation, Standard.

Vogue Pronunciation

Vogue pronunciations are not acquired by consulting the dictionary but by listening to others, who, no matter how intelligent they are, may not have the slightest idea of how to pronounce a word. The chief characteristic of vogue pronunciations is that they are adopted by those who do not want to risk being censured for sounding fussy, or different, or for lacking that great unifying quality, mediocrity.

What H. W. Fowler writes about vogue words in *Modern English Usage* applies just as well to vogue pronunciations:

> Ready acceptance of vogue-words seems to some people the sign of an alert mind; to others it stands for the herd instinct and lack of individuality . . . the second view is here taken; on the whole, the better the writer, or at any rate the sounder his style, the less will he be found to indulge in the vogue-word.

Many vogue pronunciations wind up ousting preferred pronunciations, especially if they are taken up by the broadcast media. KOH-vurt and koh-VURT, snapped up as handy companions to OH-vurt and oh-VURT, now prevail. Speakers who knew **covert** before it was battered daily on the air always pronounced it KUH-vurt. Today the vogue pronunciations SPEE-seez for **species** (properly, SPEE-sheez), FLAS-id for **flaccid** (properly, FLAK-sid), and buh-LEE-mee-uh for **bulimia** (properly, byoo-LIM-ee-uh) have detonated their petard at the doors of the dictionaries. Yet with a little boiling oil of odium, they may wither where they stand.

Selected Bibliography

Barnett, Lincoln. *The Treasure of Our Tongue*. New York: Alfred A. Knopf, 1964.

Bridgwater, William, and Seymour Kurtz, eds. *The Columbia Encyclopedia*, 3d ed. New York: Columbia University Press, 1963.

Burchfield, Robert. *The English Language*. Oxford, New York: Oxford University Press, 1986.

Ehrlich, Eugene. *Amo, Amas, Amat, and More*. New York: Harper & Row, 1985.

Follett, Wilson (ed. by Jacques Barzun, et al). *Modern American Usage*. New York: Hill & Wang, 1966.

Johnson, Samuel. *A Dictionary of the English Language*. (Facsimile of the 1755 edition.) London: Times Books, 1979.

Landau, Sidney I. *Dictionaries: The Art and Craft of Lexicography*. New York: Charles Scribner's Sons, 1984.

Mencken, H. L. *The American Language*. 4th ed. New York: Alfred A. Knopf, 1937.

Michaels, Leonard, and Christopher Ricks, eds. *The State of the Language*. Berkeley, Los Angeles, and London: University of California Press, 1980.

Morris, William, and Mary Morris. *The Harper Dictionary of Contemporary Usage*. New York: Harper & Row, 1975.

O'Connor, Johnson. *English Vocabulary Builder*. 3 vols. Boston: Human Engineering Laboratory, 1948, 1951, 1974.

Pei, Mario. *The Story of Language*. Rev. ed. Philadelphia & New York: J. B. Lippincott Company, 1965.

Simpson, D. P., ed. *Cassell's Latin Dictionary*. London: Cassell & Company Limited, and New York: Macmillan Publishing Company, 1968.

Walker, John (revised and enlarged by Lawrence H. Dawson). *The Rhyming Dictionary of the English Language*. London: George Routledge and Sons Limited, and New York: E. P. Dutton and Company, c. 1920–1930.

Webster, Noah. *Dissertations on the English Language*. 1789 Facsimile edition. Menston, Eng.: Scolar Press, 1967.

Webster, William G., and William A. Wheeler. *A Dictionary of the English Language*. Academic ed. New York and Chicago: Ivison, Blakeman & Company, and Springfield: G. & C. Merriam & Company, 1867.

Weiner, E. S. C., ed. *The Oxford Guide to English Usage*. Oxford: Clarendon Press, 1983.